China Reporting

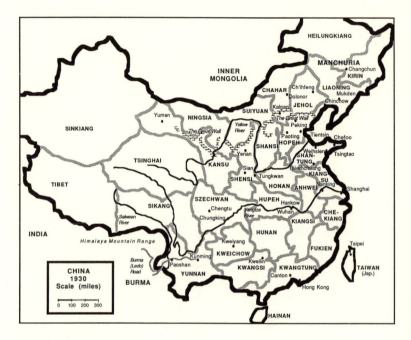

Map by Oris Friesen

China Reporting

*An Oral History of
American Journalism
in the 1930s and 1940s*

Stephen R. MacKinnon
and
Oris Friesen

UNIVERSITY OF CALIFORNIA PRESS
Berkeley   Los Angeles   London

University of California Press
Berkeley and Los Angeles, California

University of California Press, Ltd.
London, England

Printed in the United States of America
1 2 3 4 5 6 7 8 9

Library of Congress Cataloging-in-Publication Data

MacKinnon, Stephen R.
   China reporting.

   Bibliography: p.
   Includes index.
   1. Sino-Japanese Conflict, 1937–1945—Foreign
public opinion, American. 2. China—History—
Civil War, 1945–1949—Foreign public opinion,
American. 3. Foreign correspondents—United
States. 4. Foreign correspondents—China.
I. Friesen, Oris. II. Title.
DS777.533.P825U65 1987   940.53   86-19193
ISBN 0-520-05843-7 (alk. paper)

To A. T. Steele, Jr.

Contents

Preface

In the 1930s and 1940s, China attracted American journalists of all types—adventurers, missionaries, bohemians, dilettantes, serious scholars, and revolutionary activists. Their experiences and dispatches represent a vital dimension of the US–China relationship. Yet over the years, coverage of China by American journalists has received little serious retrospective analysis, perhaps because the controversial McCarthy-McCarran hearings in the 1950s clouded earlier events in China and the United States' role in them. Journalists often were made scapegoats for our "loss" of China to the Communists in 1949. Today enough time has passed to try to be more balanced. Moreover, examination of journalists' performance amidst the crises of the 1940s offers a fresh perspective on the role of the media.

How did American journalists perceive and respond to one of the most momentous events of the century—war and revolution in China during the 1930s and 1940s? How did their writing influence US policy and public opinion?

These are two of the questions that were explored at a unique gathering in Scottsdale, Arizona, during November 1982. The key figure was A. T. Steele, Jr., who is generally recognized as the dean of American reporters in

China during the 1930s and 1940s. The event was planned initially as a small gathering of a dozen "old hands" who were close to Steele. But soon the affair mushroomed and assumed a momentum of its own. By the time the meeting convened, there were more than forty veteran journalists and diplomats on hand, and also a number of distinguished scholars who study and write about this period in US-China relations.

Out of a chronological and topical distillation of what was said during and after the meeting in Scottsdale, an oral history of the journalistic experience in China during the 1930s and 1940s has been put together. In the process we have attempted to answer the questions posed above. But the focus remains limited chiefly to the experiences of those who came to Scottsdale, plus contributions from a few who were unable to attend like Jack Belden and Theodore H. (Teddy) White. In general, the speakers at Scottsdale had covered China for large American metropolitan dailies or had been wire service reporters. Although perhaps not as well known today as book and feature writers of the period like Edgar Snow and Agnes Smedley, reporters for the daily press such as A. T. Steele (*Chicago Daily News* and *New York Herald Tribune*) and Tillman Durdin (*New York Times*) were much more widely read at the time and therefore probably more influential.

Politically, considering the length of time that has elapsed and the infirmities of age, a surprisingly broad cross-section of old journalists gathered at Scottsdale. But there was one serious *lacuna.* Only Frederick Marquardt of the *Arizona Republic* represented the right or "Chiang Kai-shek" China lobby of the past (and present). Joseph Alsop was expected but was prevented at the last minute from attending by a heart attack. Doubtless, as a staunch friend of the Generalissimo and Mme. Chiang as well as of Claire Chennault, he would have attacked the "woolly liberalism" of the majority of the participants, especially their defense of General Joseph Stilwell and criticism of his sacking in 1944. This was Alsop's position on the telephone before the conference met. His absence meant that the meeting was less polemically heated than it might have been. Indeed, the participants at Scottsdale seemed to mute political differences. Their purpose in coming was to have a reunion and re-evaluate their work in professional terms. They had not come to reopen old wounds or settle scores.

We think this muting of political differences proved to be fortuitous. Without Alsop and well-worn polemics about who lost China, the myth of Communists as agrarian reformers, or the justice of Stilwell's sacking in 1944, the dynamics of reporting from Asia were explored much more thoroughly than expected. And about this—the conditions, limitations, and quality of the journalists' product itself—differences emerged which we have tried to highlight. Moreover, at the end of the conference, a number of overall assessments of the journalists' record were offered. Not surprisingly, the participants tended to be self-congratulatory. We have tried to distance ourselves from that view by weaving the veteran journalists' reminiscences into an oral history narrative that consciously balances their successes against missed stories and persistent ignorance about the fundamental changes then taking place in the Chinese countryside. The latter subject was hardly discussed at Scottsdale.

Put differently, the authors are trying to show how the China correspondent of the 1930s and 1940s constructed his or her news reality or the network of facts from which their stories were written. How these men and women pooled information and decided upon the legitimacy of particular sources is explored. The influences of competition, language facility (or lack thereof), common personal backgrounds, camaraderie, and changes in American official China policy are also discussed, with special attention paid to the prescriptive, gatekeeping role of editors back home. This is an approach which has often been applied to the domestic journalist.[1] The resulting book, it is hoped, will be considered a pioneering effort at using historical perspective to view the foreign correspondent in terms of the total epistemological context in which he or she operates to produce the news that in turn provides the data base upon which the public and policy makers inevitably draw.

By way of acknowledgments, we wish first to give special thanks to Jan MacKinnon, with whom the idea for the Scottsdale conference originated and whose encouragement was essential at crucial points along the way. Of this book's many benefactors, the most important were the financial supporters of the 1982 Scottsdale conference. Without grants from the Arizona Humanities Council, the Arizona China Council, Arizona State University's Center for Asian Studies and the Pacific Basin Institute, there would not have been a conference. Subsequently, the Arizona Humanities Council, as well as the Arizona State University grants-in-aid program, provided crucial assistance in the preparation of a manuscript. The latter was read in various drafts by McCracken Fisher, Annalee Jacoby Fadiman, Bill and Sylvia Powell, James Fisher, A. T. Steele, Jr., Orville Schell, Paul Cohen, Israel Epstein, Beth Luey, Gilbert Harrison, John Service, and Jan MacKinnon. Their help and encouragement kept the authors from becoming too discouraged about the prospects of producing a book from the transcripts of the conference. But needless to say, the interpretation of what was said at Scottsdale and its final arrangement into an oral history is solely the responsibility of the authors.

Note on Romanization and Typographic Conventions

Romanization of personal and place names in this book reflects the forms with which the journalists themselves were familiar. Wade-Giles romanization is used except for generally known place names and where idiosyncratic romanization of particular personal names was prevalent.

Throughout the text the old China hands and scholars speak directly in Roman type. Interpretation and relevant background appear in italics.

Cast of Characters

The key to following the narrative in this oral history is recognizing the participants as they speak. Listed below is our cast of characters. Attendance at the conference is noted by an asterisk (*).

Joseph Alsop

Worked with General Claire Chennault prior to Pearl Harbor; captured by Japanese in Hong Kong, repatriated and joined staff of T. V. Soong's China Defense Supplies in early 1940s. Aide to General Chennault at time of Stilwell's sacking in 1944. After the war, served as a syndicated political columnist in Washington, D.C., until his retirement.

Doak Barnett*

Born in China. Correspondent for *Chicago Daily News*, 1947–49. Author of a dozen books and today the "dean" in Washington, D.C., of academic "China watchers" as professor in the School of Advanced International Studies, Johns Hopkins University.

Jack Belden

United Press and freelance (*Saturday Evening Post*), 1937–49. Retired and living in Europe since 1950s. Author of three books on Asia, including *China Shakes the World* (1949).

Robert Blum *

Government analyst of Asian affairs; author of *Drawing the Line: The Origin of the American Containment Policy in East Asia* (1982).

Dorothy Borg *

With Institute of Pacific Relations, 1939–50 (including Shanghai, 1945–49). Historian at Columbia University and author of numerous works on US-China relations, notably *United States and the Far Eastern Crisis of 1933–38* (1964).

John Davies

China born. Served in China, 1932–44, as Foreign Service Officer and Political Adviser on staff of General Stilwell. His China experi-

	ence, including Hankow, recounted in his *Dragon by the Tail* (1972). Discharged by Dulles in 1954.
Hugh Deane*	Freelance writer, *Christian Science Monitor*, Chungking, 1940, 1944–46. Later with *Compass, Allied Labor News*; recently editor of various labor union publications. Currently, an officer of US-China Peoples' Friendship Association.
Peggy Durdin*	Daughter of China missionaries. Freelance feature writer, *Nation, Atlantic, New York Times*, 1940s to 1970s.
Tillman Durdin*	*New York Times* China correspondent, late 1930s and 1940s. Continued in Hong Kong as "dean" of American reporters on China from 1950s through 1972.
Israel Epstein*	Raised in Tientsin. United Press, *New York Times, New York Herald Tribune, Allied Labor News*, 1935–46. Returned to Peking, 1951; editor of *China Reconstructs*, 1950s to present.

Annalee Jacoby Fadiman*	Time-Life, Chungking, 1942, 1944–46. With Theodore White, author of *Thunder Out of China* (1946). Today active with husband Clifton Fadiman as Book of the Month Club editor.
John K. Fairbank*	OSS, Chungking, 1942–43; OWI, Washington, 1944–45; USIS, China, 1945–46; historian and professor at Harvard, 1940s to present. Author of half a dozen works on Chinese history, notably *The United States and China* (4 editions).
Wilma Fairbank*	Cultural attaché, American embassy, Chungking, 1945–47. Art historian: recent book, *A Pictorial History of Chinese Architecture* (1984).
F. McCracken Fisher*	Yenching University graduate in journalism, 1932; editor of *Peiping Chronicle*, 1933–35; United Press: Peking, Chungking, 1936–41. Director, OWI, China 1942–45; Department of State, 1946–50; USIA official, 1951–70.

Oris Friesen*	Historian and editor; currently an engineering fellow at Honeywell, Inc., and adjunct professor at Arizona State University.
Steven Goldstein*	Scholar, heads China Council of the Asia Society (New York). Author of *China Briefing* (1984).
Charles Hayford*	Historian and biographer of James Yen.
John Hlavacek*	Office of US Military Attaché in Chungking (Chinese language officer), 1942–44; United Press, Chungking and Burma, 1944–45; India Bureau Chief, 1945 to 1957. Television correspondent, 1960s.
Peggy Parker Hlavacek*	Freelanced in Shanghai for *New York Daily News* and other papers, 1945–49. Continued to freelance from Asia, 1950s and 1960s.
John Hersey*	Born in China. Correspondent: *Time, Life,* and *New Yorker,* 1942–46; novelist (Pulitzer Prize, 1945). Vice-president, Authors League of America (1949–55), president (1975–80); secretary, American Academy of Arts

and Letters (1962–76), chancellor (1981–84); adjunct professor emeritus, Yale. Recent work: *The Call* (1985).

Harold Isaacs

Freelance writer and editor, 1930s; author of *Tragedy of the Chinese Revolution* (1938); in 1940s Asia correspondent for *Newsweek*; professor at M.I.T., 1950s to 1970s.

Helene Keyssar*

Drama critic, teaches at University of California, San Diego. Co-author of *Right in Her Soul: The Life of Anna Louise Strong* (1983).

Don Kight*

Army Public Relations Officer: China, 1944–49; Washington, D.C., Japan, Europe, 1950s to retirement.

Harold (Hal) Levine*

Editor, *Newsweek*, 1945–50. Senior Editor, *Arizona Republic*, 1970s and 1980s.

Stephen I. Levine*

Political scientist at American University, Washington, D.C.; recent work: *Along Alien Roads: The Memoirs of a Soviet Military Advisor in China, 1938–39* (1983) by Kalyagin (translation).

Henry (Hank) Lieberman*

Editor, *Foreign News*, OWI,

	1942–45. Correspondent, *New York Times*, China, 1945–49, and for Asia, 1950s. News and science editor (*NYT*), 1957 to 1981.
Henry Luce	Son of a China missionary. Editor and founder, *Time, Life,* and *Fortune.*
Stephen R. MacKinnon*	Historian of China, teaches at Arizona State University. Co-author (with Jan Mac-Kinnon) of *Agnes Smedley: American Radical* (1987).
Frederick Marquardt*	Born in Philippines. Editor, *Free Press* (Manila), 1930s. *Chicago Sun Times*, 1949–50. Senior Editor, *Arizona Republic*, 1950s to retirement.
Pepper Martin	CBS, United Press, China, 1930s and 1940s. *U.S. News and World Report*, Senior Editor, 1950s to retirement.
John F. Melby*	American Foreign Service officer with embassy in China as political and press officer, liaison with USIS, and Director, Fulbright Foundation, 1945–50. Compiler of China White Paper (1949) and author of *The Mandate of Heaven* (1968).

Thomas Millard	Missouri newspaperman. First went to China for *New York Herald* to cover Boxer uprising in 1900. Later correspondent, *New York Times,* and editor, English-language newspaper in China, 1900–1932. Founder of *China Weekly Review* (Shanghai).
Philip Potter*	*Baltimore Sun,* 1941 to 1974: China-Burma-India Theater, 1945–46, alternating Washington, D.C., and Asian bureaus thereafter.
John B. Powell	Missouri newspaperman. First trip to China in 1917, eventually editor, *China Weekly Review,* 1928–1941, and correspondent, *Christian Science Monitor.* Captured and mistreated by the Japanese. Author of *My Twenty-five Years in China* (1945). Died 1947.
Sylvia Powell*	United Nations (UNRRA), 1945–46; China Welfare Institute, 1946–49; *China Weekly Review,* 1949–53. San Francisco businesswoman, 1950s to present.
William Powell*	Born in Shanghai. Son of J. B. Powell. *China Press,*

1940–41; Federal Commu-
nications Commission,
1942; Editor, OWI and
China Weekly Review,
1943–53, Shanghai. Feature
writer on Asian topics,
1960s to present.

Christopher Rand

China: OWI, *New York
Herald Tribune,* and *New
Yorker,* 1943–49. Died
1968.

Peter Rand*

Author of three published
works of fiction, teaches
writing at Columbia Uni-
versity. He is the son and
biographer of Christopher
Rand.

Albert Ravenholt*

United Press: China-Burma-
India, Indochina, Philip-
pines, 1943–47; *Chicago
Daily News,* 1948–69; Universities Field Staff International, 1950–present.

Marjorie Ravenholt*

OSS Intelligence, China and
India, 1943–44; *Time* and
Life, 1945–46.

Mordechai Rozanski*

Associate Provost and Director of the Center for International Studies at Adelphi
University. Historian of
Chinese-American rela-
tions, working on a history

	of American journalists in China, 1900–1929.
Harrison E. Salisbury*	United Press, 1930–48 (Foreign News Editor, 1944–48). In 1950s Soviet specialist and Moscow correspondent for the *New York Times*. Since 1960s has concentrated on Sino-Soviet and Chinese affairs. Most recent work: *The Long March: The Untold Story* (1985).
Michael Schaller*	Historian, teaches at the University of Arizona. Author of *The US Crusade in China, 1938–1945* (1979) and *The United States and China in the Twentieth Century* (1979).
Julian Schuman*	*China Press, China Weekly Review,* freelance, and ABC, Shanghai, 1947–53. Freelancer from Peking in the 1950s and 1960s. Presently with *China Daily* (Peking). Author of *Assignment China* (1956).
John S. Service*	Born in China. Foreign Service Officer, China, 1933–45. In a celebrated McCarthy case dismissed for disloyalty; eventually re-

instated in the late 1950s. *Lost Chance in China* (1974) is a collection of his key memoranda about the Chinese Communists from the 1940s.

Agnes Smedley   *Frankfurter Zeitung, Manchester Guardian*, and free-lance, China, 1929–41. Author of five books on China in the 1930s and 1940s—notably *Battle Hymn of China* (1943). Died 1950.

Gaddis Smith*   Historian, teaches at Yale University. Author of numerous works on American diplomatic history, including *Dean Acheson* (1970).

Edgar Snow   Feature writer, *Saturday Evening Post*, 1936–50. Author of *Red Star over China* (1938). Died 1972.

A. T. (Arch) Steele*   China correspondent for *New York Herald Tribune, Chicago Daily News, New York Times*, 1932–50; continued to cover Asia into the 1960s. Author of *The American People and China* (1966).

Anna Louise Strong   Journalist and revolutionary activist. Wrote for International News Service and

	freelance, 1937–49. Author of numerous works on China. Died in Peking, 1970.
Tracy Strong*	Political scientist at University of California, San Diego. Biographer of Anna Louise Strong with Helene Keyssar.
Mary Barrett Sullivan*	OWI, 1942–46; USIS, Shanghai, 1946–48; *China Weekly Review*, 1948–50. Member, Democratic National Committee since 1976, and its Executive Committee since 1980.
Walter Sullivan*	Correspondent for *New York Times* in China, 1948–50, and Berlin, 1951–56. Presently Science Editor, *New York Times* and author of three works on science.
James Thomson*	Historian, born in China, taught at Harvard and served as curator, Nieman Foundation. Currently at Boston University. Author of *While China Faced West: American Reformers in Nationalist China, 1928–1937* (1969) and *Sentimental Imperialists* (1982).
Nancy Tucker*	Historian, teaches at Colgate University. Author of

	Patterns in the Dust: Chinese-American Relations and the Recognition Controversy, 1949–1950 (1983).
James D. White*	Missouri-Yenching Fellow, Peking, 1932–35. Correspondent for Associated Press: North China, Manchuria, Mongolia, 1936–41; then editor and feature writer, San Francisco and Washington, D.C., 1942–72.
Theodore (Teddy) White	Time-Life, Chungking, 1941–46; author of numerous books, including *Thunder Out of China* (with Annalee Jacoby) (1946) and *In Search of History* (1972).
Allen Whiting*	Political scientist, teaches at the University of Arizona. Author of numerous works on China, including *China Crosses the Yalu: The Decision to Enter the Korean War* (1960 and 1968) and recently, *Siberian Development and East Asia* (1981).

Chronology

1931 September	Japan begins takeover of Manchuria.
1932 January	Chinese resist Japanese attack at Shanghai.
1935 October	Chinese Communists end Long March and establish base in North Shensi.
December	Student-led anti-Japanese demonstrations in Peking.
1936 July	Edgar Snow reaches North Shensi and ends news blockade of the Communists in effect since late 1920s.
December	Chiang Kai-shek arrested at Sian; end of anti-Communist civil war.
1937 July	Armed clash at Marco Polo Bridge near Peking begins Sino-Japanese War; Kuomintang and Communists form United Front.
December	Chinese government moves to Hankow; Japanese take and pillage Nanking.
1938 October	Hankow falls to Japanese; Chinese capital moves to Chungking.

1941 January	Kuomintang forces attack Communist New Fourth Army in central China; United Front effectively ended.
December	Bombing of Pearl Harbor brings US into the war against Japan.
1942	OWI and OSS set up and begin operations in China; US Army creates China-Burma-India Theater with General Stilwell in command.
1944 June	Party of American journalists permitted to go to Yenan; wartime news blockade of Chinese Communists ends.
July	US Army Observer Group ("Dixie") arrives at Yenan; official American contact with Communist forces begins.
September	Patrick J. Hurley arrives in Chungking as Presidential Special Representative.
October	Stilwell recalled; General Wedemeyer becomes commander of new China Theater.
1945 September	War ends; Japanese units in China ordered to surrender only to Kuomintang forces.
November	Hurley fails in mediation between Kuomintang and Communists; resigns and blames journalists and State Department officers.
December	General George C. Marshall goes to China as special envoy seeking to arrange truce and avert civil war.
1946 July	Marshall mission fails; J. Leighton

	Stuart becomes American ambassador; full-scale civil war in China.
1947 July	Wedemeyer mission to China.
1948 November	Kuomintang defenses in Manchuria collapse.
1949 January	Communists take over Peking; win decisive Huai-hai campaign.
1949 Apr.–May	Nanking and Shanghai fall.
August	State Department issues China White Paper.
October	People's Republic of China established.
1950	American journalists and officials leave China; Korean War begins; accusations by Senator McCarthy and China Lobby over "loss of China" lead to long series of Congressional investigations and charges of disloyalty against journalists, Foreign Service officers, and American scholars of China.

Introduction

JAMES THOMSON

Something astonishing and rare in American self-understanding happened recently in a most improbable setting. Some forty years after the events, the surviving reporters of the Chinese Civil War convened with a corps of historians to figure out whether (and if so, how) the press had gotten the story right. The locale was about as far as you can be from the Chinese revolution: that quintessence of the affluent Sun Belt—Scottsdale, Arizona.[1]

Journalism, it is said, is the first draft of history. But seldom do journalists submit themselves to interrogation by authors of the succeeding drafts. By then they have moved on to other stories in other parts of the forest—or perhaps out of this world entirely. Furthermore, as a group, newspeople seem skittish about admitting their role as players on the stage of history.

"War Reporting: China in the 1940s" was the title of the Scottsdale conference. How its organizers persuaded such a galaxy of reporters to participate remains something of a mystery. For more than a few, China was a bitter memory, thanks to recriminations back home as Mao Tsetung swept to victory. For others, it was a return to a subject long ago shelved. But central to the attraction, it

1

seems, was the lure of a reunion—with old friends, arch-rivals, and even former enemies. No one knew quite what to expect. A few stayed away, perhaps preferring—as one (Harold Isaacs) had put it—not to "wallow in nostalgia." But most wanted to be there in case something happened.

So there they were, some thirty-five veterans (including a few working spouses) who had reported on the China convulsion for major newspapers, magazines, and agencies (including the US government and its Office of War Information [OWI]) between the Japanese invasion in 1937 and the Communist triumph in 1949. They were joined by nearly twenty academic specialists in Sino-American relations, many of whom had written of the wartime years but knew firsthand only China of the 1970s and 1980s. These specialists had studied the documents, the output of wartime observers. But what they wanted was that elusive ingredient: what underlay those documents in the thinking and practices of the journalists.

Who were the China reporters? What kinds of "mental baggage" did they bring to China reporting? How did they operate, and who were their sources? What was their influence—in China, but especially back home in the United States?

To find the answers, the conference quickly shifted into the realm of oral history. In fairly random fashion the veterans were asked to summarize their China careers. With old memories awakening, the war years took over the hall. Anecdotes disinterred forgotten episodes; accounts were challenged or corrected, then reconfirmed; and old disagreements re-emerged, but not with rancor.

Some facts, insights, and themes emerged that can point toward answers to those large and lesser questions about wartime China reporting.

■ Most reporters came to East Asia "by accident"—as wire-service people, freelancers, or student travelers prior to 1937, or perhaps as employees of the OWI after Pearl Harbor. Virtually none had studied Chinese, and they still agree that "there is no correlation between good reporters and good linguists."

■ Many belonged (as did pioneer Edgar Snow) to the "Missouri mafia" as graduates of the University of Missouri's School of Journalism. The Missouri connection often led to employment in the Associated Press or United Press, and UP's Roy Howard was said to have a special "romantic interest" in China.

■ "Romantic" is also a word that the veterans used frequently to describe the atmosphere in the heyday of Chinese resistance to Japan, the years of the United Front between Nationalists and Communists from 1937 to 1941. In Hankow, the temporary capital after the fall of Nanking, the Romantic Era peaked. Suddenly, "we were part of the big world scene," one recalled; "we were reporters of a just cause." Before Hankow, journalists had largely worked out of that worldly Western metropolis, Shanghai; later they would molder in the Nationalists' dank far-inland hideaway, Chungking.

■ It was in Hankow that these reporters first met Chou En-lai. Chou was accessible, articulate, and charming, both in Hankow and later in Chungking. One after another, these skeptical precursors of Henry Kissinger confessed their "captivation." Even when he told untruths or something less than the truth, he commanded their admiration. ("Why," wondered Hank Lieberman, "can only high-level Communists have a sense of humor?")

■ Once lodged in Chungking, locked into a war of attrition (with the United Front in shambles), the press corps found little "romance." Nationalist propaganda was patently noncredible, while Nationalist censorship increasingly rankled. Not even Madame Chiang Kai-shek, who charmed millions on her 1943 trip to America, could obscure the realities of corruption, inflation, and mismanagement. "It was impossible to like Madame Chiang," said one who knew her well. "She had eight personalities," said another. Blockaded by Nationalist troops, Mao's capital at Yenan became for many frustrated Chungking correspondents "the Camelot of China."

■ Prior to 1937, few back in America would print (or read) the reporters' stories. China news had to relate to hometown readers—perhaps a locally-known missionary who survived a warlord shootout (while 700 Chinese did not). Also of occasional interest were tales of the Mysterious East. As "Eppie" Epstein recalled, "well after 1937, in the middle of the Pacific War, a story that got headlines in much of the American press was that the clever Chinese in Chungking, during the Lunar New Year, could make eggs stand on their small ends." To serious journalists such attitudes among editors, publishers, and readers (as well as the chronic absence of "feedback") could breed deep frustration.

■ There is, of course, the famous special case of Henry R. Luce and the China coverage of *Time* magazine. Onetime Luce protégé John Hersey brilliantly probed *Time*'s editor-in-chief's "idolatry" of the American nation, his obsession with China and anti-Communism, and his use of Foreign Editor Whittaker Chambers to alter the dispatches of *Time*'s field correspondents. Hersey's testimony was confirmed by others who had experienced Chambers's transformation of fact into "total fiction."

■ One key revelation was the degree of "sympathy and cooperation" prevailing then among reporters and US officials, the press, and the government, in covering the China story. A diplomat said: "It was a continual game, finding out what was going on"; and essential to the task was "a sharing of information," a two-way exchange.

■ After Pearl Harbor the press-government partnership was strengthened by the journalists' need for logistical support. US military and civilian officials provided a vital network of communications for dispatches as well as planes and other facilities. Such cooperation in the field continued even after the Pacific War ended and the Chinese Civil War began anew. Also continuing was the customary exchange of information, and sometimes consultations of journalists by high-level officials.

■ 1945 was, however, a watershed. With the death of FDR, a new group came to power in Washington. And in China, General Patrick Hurley, the Republican ambassador, resigned, firing off a salvo of charges alleging pro-Communism and disloyalty among State Department and embassy staff, charges that would help polarize American politics in the coming Cold War and make China policy a poisonous issue for years. Inevitably China reporters were caught in the crossfire. At Scottsdale there were three (the Powells and Julian Schuman) who were indicted for sedition, then treason, but won their case after seven years.

■ On the matter of General Hurley, regarded by many as the godfather of McCarthyism, one moment of drama was the credible account by Annalee Jacoby of the ambassador's advanced senility. An empty-headed Hurley was familiar to many; but Hurley demented was something new and troubling, for this was a man who shaped history by trying to "mediate" between Mao and Chiang Kai-shek.

■ Were the reporters biased in favor of the Chinese Communists? The answer from the veterans was, "No." They were all aware, they said, of efforts by both sides to manipulate them; their common denominator was skepticism. They reported what they saw and knew. Nonetheless, as one put it, "in China, and later Vietnam, we knew all the seaminess of the right-wing groups; but we knew nothing of the seaminess of the revolutionary side." As another cautioned, one must distinguish between American journalists' attitudes toward revolutionaries "before and after they achieve power." A. T. Steele recalled one interesting dilemma: how to report good things about the Communists without appearing pro-Communist to an American reading public that was traditionally anti-Communist. "One possible stratagem," he suggested, "was to deny that the Chinese Communists were 'real Communists.'"

The China war reporters of nearly forty years ago inevitably wondered how well they had done. Historian John Fairbank offered a somber response: "We all tried, but we failed, in one of the great failures of history. We could not educate or communicate. We were all superficial—academics, government officials, journalists. We were a small thin stratum. . . . We never talked to a peasant."

The Fairbank view ran counter to the general sentiment. "All told," Henry Lieberman concluded, "we did a pretty goddamn good job."

1   Henry Luce and the Gordian Knot

The single most influential journalist who wrote or edited about China in the 1940s was undoubtedly Henry Luce. As centers of power, prestige, and money, his Time-Life publications attracted top talent. About China and Chiang Kai-shek in particular, Luce was strongly opinionated and, when speaking through foreign editor Whittaker Chambers, avidly anti-Communist. Conflict between Luce and his talented reporters in the field was inevitable and well illustrates the overall problems the China journalist faced in getting the news published as he/she saw it. The forced departure from Time-Life in 1944–45 of T. H. White and John Hersey mirrored the confrontations that were occurring in the State Department at the same time between Foreign Service officers in the field like John Service and John Davies and Washington politicians-turned-diplomats such as Patrick Hurley. The result was a double tragedy, producing over the rest of the decade both an indecisive US China policy and uncertain coverage of the Chinese Civil War. For these reasons, the Luce story is essential background for an understanding of the increasingly politicized editorial environment in America that shaped press coverage of China in the 1940s. It also raises basic questions about relationships between the US government and the American press in regard to China, which are pursued throughout the rest of the book.

There was probably no one who knew Henry Luce better in terms of his thoughts on China in the early 1940s than John Hersey, one-time Luce protégé and later Pulitzer Prize winning author. One of the high points of the Scottsdale meeting was Hersey's luncheon address on Henry Luce which follows.

Henry Luce underwent a profound change between 1937 and 1948. These were the years of his greatest involvement with China. I was his employee during all but the last three of those years.

When I first went to work for him at *Time*, at $35 a week, he seemed a walking wonder of possibilities to a *mishkid* like me—a missionary offspring, that is. He was a mishkid who had made good in a big way. He was exciting to be around. Emotions—feelings that had to do with a human touch—were enigmatic in him, but abstractions lit up his face, as if in a dazzling *son et lumière* at the Sphinx. His mind darted and jumped. He was astonished and delighted by whatever he had not previously known. He stammered because so many enthusiasms were trying to make simultaneous escape across his Calvinist tongue. Because I, too, was a China mishkid, he would in those earlier days call me up to the thirty-third floor, now and then, to discuss a China story. This was great. Together we would explore a dozen approaches. Then he would say, "Go and write it"—and it would be for me to choose which of the approaches to use.

By the end of the period, it was another and much more terrible case. A conference on a story would begin, "John, the way I see this thing is. . . ." Sometimes his commands or correctives were in memo form, in prose hewn by a chilled axe. It got so bad that, on receiving one of Luce's lightning bolts, T. S. Matthews, as managing editor, wrote back: "No decent human being would answer your memo by accepting it. . . . You have written as if to dogs, not to human beings. And you have made a mistake. If you're really degenerating into a barking boss, you'll soon have behind you only the anxious, stupid, dishonest subservience that kind of boss can command."[1]

We all know in a general way how Henry Luce's views on China moved and hardened in those years. Early we find him urging resistance to China's enemy, Japan; deploring American sales of scrap steel to the Japanese; warmly praising progressive undertakings like the Chinese Industrial Cooperatives founded by the New Zealander Rewi Alley. Next he is an Asia-firster, with growing differences with Roosevelt on the conduct of the war. Then he writes a personal letter to every subscriber to *Time* asking for support of United China Relief. Next he is squarely in the pro-Chiang China Lobby. And finally, in 1948, he is the bitter author of a letter to Senator Arthur Vandenberg: "The measure of the degradation of American policy in the Pacific is the fact that a few guys like Representative Walter H. Judd and I have to go about peddling a vital interest of the United States and a historic article of US foreign policy as if it were some sort of bottled chop suey that we were trying to sneak through the Pure Food Laws."[2]

Now here is an intriguing question: Why did that particular missionary son reach a destination on the China question so very different from that reached by other sons of missionaries—notably, for a couple of examples, John Paton Davies and John Service? These two mishkids were hounded out of the Foreign Service by Senator Joseph McCarthy for the sin of seeing the China picture, as we know

now, far more accurately than Henry Luce was seeing it. Why the difference?

First of all, there was the matter of Henry Robinson Luce's foremost model and mentor—his father, Henry Winters Luce, called, as his son was to be, Harry. I have been working for about four years on a fictional biography of a missionary in China. I have done a great deal of research, and I must say I have found no other missionary figure quite like Harry Luce the First. He was a wheeler and dealer. He thought big; the minute he saw a small missionary college, he wanted it to be a university. He had a life-long romance, sometimes stormy, with money. It was his fate to be, not a soulsaver, but a fundraiser. Sherwood Eddy, who roomed with Luce and Horace Pitkin at Union Theological Seminary before they went out, tells that one night the three of them talked so fervently about money that in bed later he dreamed he saw a hand up near the ceiling holding a fistful of cash; he leaped out of bed to reach for it and crashed to the floor. Of the senior Luce's thirty years as a missionary, he spent eleven back in the States raising money for Tengchow College, Cheeloo University, and Yenching University, for the last of which he attracted more than $2 million.

This money man instilled a hot ambition in his son. "Character is destiny," he kept telling him.[3] And his constant exhortation to young Henry was "Use your native Lucepower."[4] At about twelve years of age the son wrote home from Chefoo School: "I would like to be Alexander if I were not Socrates."[5] Early on, father Harry had made connections that would pay off in son Harry's career. The headmaster of the tiny Scranton private school he went to was Walter H. Buell, later to be headmaster of the Hotchkiss School, which the younger Harry would attend. The wealthy Scranton businessman who put up the entire support for the father's mission was James A. Linen, whose grandson would later show up as president of Time, Inc. Mrs. Cyrus McCormick, widow of the inventor of the harvester, built a house for the father in Weihsien and years later gave the son a thousand-dollar gift on his graduation from Yale, which made it possible for him to take a year of graduate study at Oxford.

Here is an interesting fact, for what it's worth: Harry Luce the elder went out to China before the Boxer uprising of 1900; the fathers of Davies and Service went out after it. Luce *père* escaped to Korea, but his close friend Horace Pitkin was killed in Paotingfu. I touch glancingly on this fact because the Boxer time appears to me to have been the watershed between two quite different breeds of missionaries—the dedicated evangelists before it, and the slightly more worldly social-gospel missionaries, who wanted to help improve the quality of life for the Chinese, after it. This difference may have been reflected in the outlooks of the sons.

At any rate, religion seems to have been more tenacious in Luce than in Service and Davies; he held on to his Presbyterianism, while they seem to have been in varying degree apostate. "An ample road to salvation was marked out for me in childhood," he once said.[6] He was baptized by one of the craggy giants of the Protestant church in China, Dr. Calvin Mateer; and that wet touch on his forehead left a kind of scald that stayed hot under his skin all his life long. His sister Beth has an early memory of his standing on a stool in the mission compound preaching a sermon to *amahs* and babies. Among the family papers there is a sermon he wrote, at age six, on 2 Timothy 1:7: "For God hath not given us the spirit of fear." His faith was not always easy. More than once he said in the presence of colleagues, "O Lord, I believe—help Thou my unbelief." It was clearly understood by all of us that Luce should be allowed to ride alone in the elevator each day up to and down from his office, and he confided to a very few friends that he spent those few minutes of daily ascension and fall in prayer.

Luce's editorial associate John Jessup wrote some years ago:

> John Courtney Murray made a curious point in reflecting on his Protestant friend's "astonishing and all but unclassifiable" mind. It was that many of the serious thinkers to whom Luce was most attracted—Hocking, Toynbee, Tillich, Haering, and later Teilhard de Chardin—were all what Murray called "gnostics." By this Murray did not mean that they were followers of the second-century heresy. He meant that they were all semi-mystic followers of personal paths to truth who put more of their puzzled faith in intuition than in revelation or authority. "Poor indeed is the unmystical philosophy," wrote Luce in college, and he never ceased to believe in the possibility of private visions of God. Yet he could not himself be called a gnostic. His own religion was less mystical than historical, rooted in time and place.
>
> It was rooted in Palestine in the first three decades A.D. This historical event, as Luce saw it, was the high point of God's intervention in human affairs that began with the Creation, picked up speed with Abraham, left signs for the eye of faith in every century, and will make its purpose fully clear at the end of the world. Luce's providential view of history remained intact against the arguments of his more learned and less certain friends.[7]

Pressed once about his rigidity on some issue, Luce rather testily blurted out: "I *am* biased in favor of God, the Republican party, and free enterprise."[8] What is interesting here is the interconnection of those biases. For Henry Luce held to a Presbyterian interpretation of history. In a speech at the centennial of Lake Forest College in Illinois in 1957 he said: "[What] I want to emphasize tonight is that God is the ruler of human history. We need not," he said, "exaggerate the dominance of Calvinist influence in the founding of the United States. Enough to say that Presbyterians played an immense part in it—and without the Calvinist influence, the American form of government and the American ethos are inconceivable." And he went on: "God moves in a mysterious way. Who would have thought that He would have dedicated the New World, the new hope of mankind, to freedom, by the means of such ornery people as us Presbyterians. But the record is there—facts are facts." He also said in that speech: "Presbyterians are credited with the invention of modern capitalism—and if we accept the credit, as we might as well, we are accountable for the horrible sins of capitalism as well as for the revolutionary advance of human productivity and physical well-being."[9]

Thus, he could account for his own fast-growing material well-being as God-sent—though he knew that some thought him in touch with Mammon. He was aware, and hurt, that certain clergymen considered his publications materialistic and unprincipled; his mother let him know she was worried about his immortal soul because, among other reasons, he presided over what was then the world's largest medium for the advertising of alcoholic beverages.

The younger Luce's connection with money was far closer than his father's. His father raised it; he made it. Of course this distinction sharply marks off Henry R. Luce from Davies and Service, and indeed from other mishkids in general. Lucepower, it turned out, was money power; such influence as the other two gained and later lost was manifestly not material. At Hotchkiss, where Luce waited on tables and swept out classrooms as a scholarship student, he thought of becoming a businessman in China— as he put it at the time, in "some big economic movement—railroads, mining, wholesale farming, 5- and 10-cent stores, news syndicates."[10] He seemed to think of this opportunity as a kind of mission in itself, because, as he wrote, "before the [Chinese] people as a whole become alive to the 'higher things' they must get their noses off the economic grindstone."[11] Someone once called Luce "the very embodiment of Max Weber's Protestant ethic,"[12] one who must have agreed with Victorian divines that "God is in league with riches." Be that as it may, by the beginning of the period we are talking about, Luce held shares of Time, Inc., stock worth on paper more than $20 million, and not yet forty years old, he drew dividends from them, as the Depression dwindled away, of something like $800,000 a year. Nineteen-thirties dollars.

The money power was, of course, ancillary to his growing power as an editor. He became sure of himself. He had not always been. At Hotchkiss and Yale, the boy who had wanted to be an Alexander—you will remember that whoever untied the Gordian knot would rule all of Asia, and books said that Alexander had cut the knot with a single daring blow of his sword—this young dreamer suffered the humiliation of being second in magnetism, popularity, and power to his friend Britten Hadden, who was chosen over Luce to be editor first of the Hotchkiss *Record* and later of the *Yale Daily News.* At school and college, Luce had the hated nickname "Chink." College life was a bit heavy. Sardonic Hadden, meeting Luce one day on the campus, called to him, "Watch out, Harry, you'll drop the college." When the two founded *Time,* Hadden again got the top spot, as editor. At the height of prosperity in the late twenties, Luce wanted to start a magazine on business, to which he wanted to give the name *Power.* Hadden was opposed, but in 1929, at age thirty-one, he considerately died, and Luce at last became top dog as editor of *Time.* He was now free to found *Fortune;* and on the eve of the period we are considering, he had just started the fabulously successful *Life.*

In this period of change, there was one constant in Luce. At a dinner of *Time* editors he said: "I regard America as a special dispensation—under Providence. . . . My spiritual pastors shake their heads about this view of mine. They say it tends to idolatry—to idolatry of nation."[13] Luce's particular strain of patriotism was fixed in him early. Speaking to *Time*'s so-called Senior Group of executives on another occasion, he told of going, at age ten, to the Chefoo School, where only about a fifth of the students were American. "We were," he said, "a strong, conspicuous, successful minority [among which, by the way, was Thornton Wilder]. The British code—flogging and toadying—violated every American instinct. No wonder that hardly an hour passed that an American did not have to run up the flag. A master insists that Ohio is pronounced O-hee-ho. What are you going to do? Will you agree? The American can't agree; it would betray every other American. So first your knuckles are rapped, then you get your face slapped—by the master—then you are publicly caned. By this time you are crying, but still you can't say O-hee-ho."[14]

"In some ways," Luce said, in 1950, "that background endowed me with special qualifications to be editor-in-chief of great American publications. . . . In some ways, it disqualified me. I probably gained a too romantic, too idealistic view of America. The Americans I grew up with—all of them—were good people. Missionaries have their faults, but their faults are comparatively trivial. I had no experience of evil in terms of Americans. . . . Put along with that the idea that America was a wonderful country, with opportunity and freedom and justice for all, and you got not only an idealistic, but a romantic view—a profoundly false romantic view."[15]

This insight may have come as hindsight, for it was uttered long after the public reaction to his famous essay "The American Century," published in 1941. Reading it now, one sees a distinctly pre-Boxer tension of opposites in it. First there is this: "We must now," he wrote, "undertake to be the Good Samaritan of the entire world. It is the manifest duty of this country to undertake to feed all the people of the world who . . . are hungry and destitute. . . . For every dollar we spend on armaments, we should spend at least a dime in a gigantic effort to feed the world. Every farmer in America should be encouraged to produce all the crops he can, and all that we cannot eat—and perhaps some of us could eat less—should forthwith be dispatched to the four quarters of the globe as a free gift, administered by a humanitarian army of Americans, to every man, woman, and child on this earth who is really hungry." On the other side of the coin there is this in the essay: "We have to decide whether or not we shall have for ourselves and our friends freedom of the seas—the right to go with our ships and our oceangoing airplanes where we wish, and when we wish, and as we wish. . . . Our thinking on world trade today is on ridiculously small terms. For example, we think of Asia as being worth only a few hundred million a year to us. Actually, in the decades to come, Asia will be worth to us exactly zero—or else it will be worth to us four, five, ten billion dollars a year. And the latter are the terms we must think in, or else confess a pitiful impotence."

Luce was right in saying that his romantic Americanism had been planted in him early. I have come across a fascinating preview of "The American Century." Partly, no doubt, because of his stammer—or rather because when he spoke forensically he did not stammer—he set great store by oratory in his school and college years. Winning the DeForest Oration Prize at Yale in 1920, he pronounced these amazingly predictive words, which he very nearly plagiarized from himself word for word in "The American Century": "When we say 'America' twenty years from now may it be that the great name will signify throughout the world at least two things: first, that American interests shall be respected, American citizens entitled to trade and to live in every corner of the globe, American business ideals recognized wherever the trader goes; second, that America may be counted upon to do her share in every international difficulty, that she will be the great friend of the lame, the halt and the blind among nations, the comrade of all nations that struggle to rise to higher planes of social and political organization, and withal the implacable and *immediate* foe of whatever nation shall offer to disturb the peace of the world. If this shall be, then the America of this century shall have glory and honor to take into that City of God far outshining the glory and honor which the kings do bring."[16]

Three months after the publication of "The American Century," Luce went to China, and in Chungking he extended his idolatry of nation to embrace also the one—or the part of one—presided over by the Christian Chiang Kai-shek and the Christian Soong Mei-ling, Chiang's wife. During that visit he also encountered and was dazzled, charmed, and challenged by the brilliant young *Time* correspondent there, Theodore H. White. On his return to the States he took White with him, to make him an editor of the magazine—but, more important, to adopt him, to take possession of him. As he had done, in a different but no less paternal way, over the years, with me. Four years later, both White and I had, not without pain, torn ourselves away from him.

At this point I should probably remind you of two people who had a great deal to do with the change in Luce during the years we are talking about. The first, of course, was Clare Boothe, whom he had married two years before this period began. Her diamond-hard mind and her religious journey toward Rome, which culminated in her conversion just at the height of White's and my struggles with Luce, certainly bore on his views on China. Her conversion to Catholicism could not have been easy for him, this faithful Presbyterian missionary's son, but he accepted it with Calvinist fortitude. Clare reinforced his bias in favor of God and against the Godless. In an interview with *McCall's* she said the experience of her conversion had given her increased moral ammunition against the Communists—because of their denial of personal sin.

The other person, who figured much more directly in the White and Hersey outcomes, was Whittaker Chambers. He had joined the *Time* staff in 1939, the year after his renunciation of the Communist party, and he had become the Foreign News Editor. By late 1944 the monotone of paranoia he imposed on *Time*'s foreign news had begun to alarm not only White in China and me in Moscow but also Walter Graebner in London, Charles Wertenbaker in Paris, John Osborne in Rome, and others. "Some recent copies of *Time* have just reached me," I cabled Tom Matthews one week. "In all honor I must report to you that I do not like the tone of many Foreign News stories. I need not itemize: You know what I mean . . . for this week, and until I cool off, I shall abstain from corresponding with Foreign News."

This was also the juncture at which Teddy White sent back from China a long and considered account of the firing of Stilwell, which he managed to have flown home on Stilwell's plane. When he read a Domei summary of the cover story Chambers wrote on Stilwell, White blew up, threatened to quit, and flew off to Yenan.

There were so many complaints like these that Luce ordered a survey of a number of correspondents' opinions of Chambers's editing. A query was sent to us in the field. The replies were unanimous. All cabled back essentially what I cabled back: Passages used from my dispatches were "torn from the context . . . and put into [the] new context of *Time's* editorial bias," which, I said, "was grossly unfair" and "actually vicious."

In the very midst of all this, Luce, with his fits of charm and seduction, cabled me offering to bring me home and train me for the top job on the magazine, the managing editorship—just as he had taken Teddy White home to make him what he could never be, an editor. I declined, asserting that I was a writer and that I would anyway have been a prickly choice, in view of his bias in favor of the Republican party and the fact that I was a convinced Democrat.

Luce soon circularized the correspondents with his judgment of their replies to the survey, and there was no doubt where he came out. "The posture of events in January, 1945," he cabled, "seems to have confirmed Editor Chambers about as fully as a news-editor is ever confirmed. . . . I have just been told, in a highly confidential manner, that Stalin is, after all, a Communist. I am also somewhat less confidentially informed that the Pope is a Christian. Some will say: what does it matter in either case? And what does it matter that Hersey advises me that he, John Hersey, is a Democrat? Well, I cannot say for sure just what these pieces of information signify, but one must respect the data in each case. A good Foreign News Editor, while guarding against the prejudices arising from his own convictions, will not ignore the circumstance that the Pope is a Christian and Stalin a Communist and Hersey, God bless him, a Democrat."[17]

Cryptic stuff—but the message was clear. So far as the boss was concerned, Chambers was right and the men in the field were wrong. Take it or leave it.

In February, Teddy White sent a cable about a new breakdown of negotiations between the Nationalists and Communists; Chambers used not a word of the dispatch. White quarrelled along until April. Luce was evidently shaken by Teddy's arguments, because he wrote a memo to his management executive committee advising them "of the possible serious error of my policy in Red China." He went on: "For myself, barring details of execution, I have not the slightest doubt that [Time's] policy has been right. . . . Nevertheless, it is in some respects a dangerous policy to pursue and I shall be glad to receive from you advice and counsel thereon."[18] The committee did not ask for a change, and soon Luce sent White an extraordinary message through a third party: "After consultation with Luce," the cable said, "here's what he (and most emphatically he) would like you to do: stay in and near Chungking . . . to report not political China . . . [but] mainly small indigenous colorful yarns." As a sample of the kind of reportage Luce expected of him, the editor sent an excerpt of a London bureau cable on England's two-thousandth day of war: "Yellow crocuses bloomed, daffodils sold for dollar and a half per bunch, Commons passing bill making rear lights compulsory on bicycles."[19] Till the end of the war White limited himself to reporting on the fighting. In his book *In Search of History,* he tells movingly of the final break on his return to the States, when Luce put to him, in effect, the question: "Will you do whatever I tell you to do as my employee?" Teddy said, "No," and that was that.

Just about then I left *Time* and went to China and Japan on contracts with strange bedfellows, *Life* and *The New Yorker. The New Yorker* asked me to do a story on the damage in Hiroshima; *Life* made no such suggestion. Several years later I saw Luce walking toward me on a sidewalk in New York. He saw me, and it was clear that he intended to cut me dead. I blocked his way and spoke to him, however, and I found that he was still furious at my disloyalty in not having given the Hiroshima story to *Life.* He and I came to quite different reasons for wishing there had never been an atom bomb. In an unpublished book he was working on at the time of his death he wrote:

> If the bomb had not been dropped and if the well-laid plans for the MacArthur invasion had been carried out—then, almost certainly, the following would have occurred on the mainland of China. In September–October of 1945 there would have been a major Chinese offensive, with American-trained Chinese divisions, leading out of the mountain fastness and down to Canton. It would have been successful. Then, during the winter, having regrouped around Canton, the Generalissimo would have marched north and taken the Yangtze Valley as he had done twenty years before. If the Japanese had then surrendered in the spring of 1946, Chiang Kai-shek would have been in a position to move armies up to Peking and Manchuria. He would still have had to face the Mao Tse-tung trouble . . . but Chiang would have had a chance—and I think he deserved that chance.

And so Henry Robinson Luce had reached his final destination in a wish: That the sword could have done it. That Alexander, who cut the Gordian knot, could have made the dream come true. For it had all become a dream. He spoke to the Senior Group of Time, Inc., once about his revisit in 1945 of Tsingtao, which he said was "the most beautiful of all places on this earth, where the mountains come down to the sea. Kaiser Wilhelm II called it the fairest jewel in his crown. It was the last grab of European imperialism in Asia. . . . All I wanted was to swim on the beaches of the bay. And I did. And I took with me the finest swimmer in the United States Marine Corps, Major General [Lemuel] Shepherd. I tell you very solemnly, if American affairs had been entrusted to Major General Shepherd and me, China would not now be Communist."[20]

2 | The Shanghai Scene in the 1930s

Henry Luce and his protégés in the field, T. H. White and John Hersey, did not exist in a historical vacuum. Preceding them was an American press involvement in China which is not as well known. A key figure was Thomas Franklin Fairfax Millard, who began covering events in China in the early 1900s. As a contemporary of Henry Luce's father, Millard shared the pre-Boxer zeal of both Luces for creating a special paternalistic relationship between the United States and China. Historian Mordechai Rozanski considers Millard the founding father of American journalism in China. Rozanski continues:

Millard was an adventurer, a romantic, a muckraker, and a progressive. He had a sense of mission that many who lived in the Midwest and Missouri carried with them into the world. He had read expansionists Captain Alfred Thayer Mahan, Albert J. Beveridge, and Brooks Adams. He was a war correspondent at the turn of the century and his experiences in the Boer, Greco-Turkish, Spanish-American and Russo-Japanese wars convinced him that America had a special role to play in the Far East. He believed not only that he should stake his future career on reporting about China, but that he personally could play a major role in American policy toward China.

From 1900 to 1930, Millard wrote seven books and reported for the *New York Times, New York World, New York Herald, New York Herald Tribune, Scribner's, Nation*, and others. Because it was a time of political transition in China characterized by disorder and lack of authority, Millard and those associated with him were able to engage effectively in advocacy journalism. But he quickly realized that the American public was not very interested in China, that editors stood in the way of getting the word out and educating the public. So he sought to influence the foreign policy elite, and in this task he was helped by friends with influence and money, such as Charles Crane, an influential Chicagoan who, after making a great deal of money, devoted his life to pushing the concept of a special US relationship with China and Asia. Millard was often subsidized by Crane to the tune of $500 a month, and at times by various Chinese governments. Besides writing, Millard went to Washington to try to influence the State Department and constituent groups such as missionaries and businessmen, relentlessly propounding the idea of a special relationship with China.

Millard failed in part because China was not a central concern to American interests. But in terms of influence on other journalists, Millard was more successful. It is interesting to see how many journalists from the Midwest in later periods developed similar motivations. Many had that same sense of mission, a willingness to advocate a particular view and a particular role for the United States and China. Not really understanding China very deeply, Millard used China as an instrument, as an object for achieving what he believed to be American goals. To a certain extent, he significantly influenced a later generation of reporters whom I like to call the Missouri mafia.

Millard was the godfather figure. He was a graduate of the University of Missouri and an enthusiastic supporter of its School of Journalism. Of the fifty University of Missouri journalism graduates who came out to the Far East during the 1920s and 1930s, thirty stayed on in China. They came out in part because of Millard, but also because of another influential figure, B. W. Fleisher, who ran the *Japan Advertiser* and maintained a special relationship with the Missouri school. Among these Missouri grads was Edgar Snow, who came to China in 1928, and later acknowledged his debt to Millard's "anti-colonial, anti-imperialist, pro-independence, pro-equality of nations, pro-Republican, pro-self-determination and very pro-American [views.]."[1]

In response to Rozanski, Bill Powell offered a different picture of Millard, the Missouri connection, and his father, J. B. Powell, who ran the principally American-owned weekly China Weekly Review *in Shanghai in the 1920s and 1930s.*

I think that it is not entirely balanced to give Millard and B. W. Fleisher, who worked for Millard in establishing the *China Press* prior to moving on to Japan, almost sole responsibility for the Missouri connection. Millard was the main originator—he brought my father to China— but the real operation of Rozanski's "Missouri mafia" was in the hands of others, such as my father, Morris Harris (AP), John Morris (UP), Vic Keene (*NY Herald Tribune*) et al., and, perhaps more important, Chinese returned students from Missouri, such as Hollington Tong, who had been a student of Dad's at the Journalism School (Missouri).

Of equal importance was the fact that they were aided—actually directed—by Dean Walter Williams, the founder of the Journalism School and an unbelievable practitioner of public relations. He kept his graduates involved and in line. Over the years Dad received a continuous stream of letters from the Dean, "suggesting" that he do this or that, that he get the grads moving, almost always on something the Dean felt would promote the school. The American and Chinese Missouri graduates turned the Dean's later visit to China into a major personal and media triumph, rather like that of a visiting head of state.

The Dean concentrated on Dad because they were closer. Dad had been a graduate of the first Journalism School class (1910) and later returned to teach under the Dean, which was what he was doing when Millard asked the Dean to send him as an assistant.

About Millard, I only knew him in his later years, but he was still very much of a personality, elegant, white haired, charismatic, belting down martinis, and chasing and being chased. He was always charming and considerate to me. Dad was very fond of him and always said he learned a lot from Tommy, but also discovered early that he was difficult to work with.

Millard had brought Dad out to help him start the *Review* in 1917. Soon he sold out to Dad. I suspect he was not cut out to be an editor, the desk was probably too confining and his hellish temper and stubbornness (dedication, perhaps "advocacy") always alienated advertisers and sooner or later just about everybody else. He was a very interesting man and, like most of us, a bit complex.

Another way the Missouri School of Journalism influenced Chinese and American journalism was through its close relationship with the Department of Journalism at Yenching University in Peking. The Yenching journalism faculty included many Missouri graduates and teaching fellows. In 1932 the dean of Missouri's School of Journalism, Frank L. Martin, was an exchange professor at Yenching and virtual department head. Mac Fisher, who graduated from Yenching's Department of Journalism in 1933, was one of the products of this direct influence.

My first day in China I went to the funeral of Chang Tso-lin, in July 1928. His funeral was occasioned by his death. His death was occasioned by the Japanese military blowing up the train in which Chang, the so-called warlord of Manchuria, was returning from Peking. Early in my life in China, therefore, I was impressed by the fact of Japanese aggression. I was on a student tour of the Orient at the time. Chang Tso-lin's eldest son and successor, Chang Hsueh-liang, gave a banquet as part of the funeral ceremonies. He told us that he was going to throw in his lot—that is, Manchuria—with the Nationalist government, which was then coming to the climax of its northern expedition, and that if we saw Chiang Kai-shek we were to tell him that Manchuria would be with the Nationalist government. It was not going to separate and become subject to Japanese direction. The next week we were in Peking. Chiang arrived with his new bride, Soong Mei-ling, and gave us an interview in which we passed along Chang Hsueh-liang's message.

As a student at Yenching University from 1931 through 1933, I had participated in some of the anti-Japanese demonstrations. As a correspondent, I covered the December

9, 1935, student demonstrations. One of the leaders was my Yenching schoolmate Huang Hua. All these demonstrations were directed against Japanese aggression. "Fan-tui Jih-pen ti-kuo chu-i (Oppose Japanese imperialism)" was the shouted demand.

On July 7, 1937, as United Press correspondent for North China, I went to the Marco Polo Bridge with Colonel Joseph Stilwell, then the American military attaché, to observe the results of the Japanese attack that began Japan's eight-year effort to conquer China.

As journalists in the 1930s, we reported the news as carefully as we could, but the main inspiration of those who were there before 1941 was outrage over the fact of Japanese aggression. Perhaps there was a parallel with those who watched events in Europe as the Axis started its aggression in the mid-1930s.

With Fisher in Peking during the early 1930s was James D. White, another Missouri graduate. Both were learning the ropes as journalists by working on English-language dailies in North China. White recalls:

Just after arriving in Peking in 1932, I had been dunked into an extraordinarily educational situation. I was supposed to be an exchange graduate student and teacher at Yenching University, but the Department of Journalism had moved the campus weekly newspaper into Peking. They converted it into a daily, after the only English-language daily in town had been closed down by a warlord who was on the outs with its sponsors in Nanking.

Mac Fisher (later my UP competition in Peking) had been editing this transplanted *Yenching Gazette* and now had to finish up the course work for his degree. So, to my horror, they made me the new editor in spite of my greenness and ignorance. But with world news copy pouring in from British, French, German, American, Russian, Chinese, and Japanese news agencies, the whole thing turned into a fascinating crash course in international affairs. If you shook down all these various viewpoints, noting contradictions and sorting out motives, you could see through the propaganda pitches and discern the truth, or something very close to it. This lasted more than a year, until the Nationalist government got its Peking daily going again, and I emerged with a global perspective and a healthy insight into propaganda scams that I cannot imagine picking up in such a short time anywhere else.

It was not Missouri but the Great Depression that brought Archibald Trojan Steele to China in the early 1930s. What initially impressed Steele, like Fisher, was Japanese aggression against China.

I owned a small weekly newspaper in California when the Japanese invaded Manchuria beginning September 18, 1931. Up to that moment I had had no interest whatever in China. My sole interest was in the orange crop around Downey, California, where I was working, and in trying to keep my head above water. In fact, the Depression was bankrupting me, and I decided I had to find some other outlet. The headlines about China in the newspapers attracted me. I turned my newspaper over to my business manager, collected what cash I could, and boarded a ship named *Taiyo Maru* for Shanghai without knowing a thing about China, without any job in prospect, and only hoping that I could get into the center of the excitement.

Fortunately, I arrived in China just before the Japanese attack on Shanghai, and I was therefore able to obtain a job very quickly. For a newcomer without much idealism, it was a very good situation to get into, because Shanghai in those days was an international city with its International Settlement and French Concession and a very large and lively Chinese population. So one could get a very quick education. It might not all be accurate, but it would certainly teach you in a very short time to take a strong position on China.

Among the resident foreigners, the prevailing question in those days was: What's wrong with China? After about two weeks in Shanghai watching the Japanese and the Chinese fight back and forth, I knew the answer. Over the ensuing years, of course, that went through many modifications. But it was a very convenient war for a neophyte to cover because you could be on one side in the morning watching the Japanese bombing Chapei and Hongkew, the parts of Shanghai that were most involved in the fighting. In the afternoon you could go to the other side of the lines and talk to the commander of the Chinese forces at Shanghai, who put up a brilliant defense at a time when the Chinese were being generally maligned as very poor fighters. Indeed, at the time he was rather an exception to the rule.

Professor Rozanski has suggested that after about 1932 a more sophisticated breed of correspondent showed up in China. Unfortunately, I missed getting into the privileged category by exactly one week. I arrived in the last week of December 1931 and in a very short time met some very interesting colleagues who, like myself, truly belonged to the tribe of the ignorant who had been hustled over from the United States. Many could well be described as muckrakers and adventurers. One of them was Floyd Gibbons, the great headline hunter. He worked for the Hearst newspapers and was always out for a big, exclusive story. It might not always be correct, but it was going to be big and exclusive. He was sending them in, too, in machine gun order until one day his stories stopped reaching the home office. This precipitated a telegram from New York to another correspondent after Gibbons had been missing for three days, asking, "Where is Gibbons?" A friendly, or you might say unfriendly, correspondent responded promptly, "In barroom, Palace Hotel, shall I cover?" That's the way I got my start in China. Later I joined the field staff of the *New York Times*, then led by Hallett Abend, their chief correspondent in Shanghai, who was a good correspondent, though his leanings were certainly pro-Japanese. He gave me a job in Manchuria at the magnificent salary of $50 a month.

Shortly after my arrival, I was given a great story. I was to find Ma Chan-shan, a Chinese warlord who had joined up with the Japanese as a puppet minister of war in the Manchukuo government. Another correspondent and I, the other being August Lindt of the Swiss *Journal de Genève*, cooked up the project of going back into the interior behind the Japanese lines to find Ma, with whom the Lytton Commission of the League of Nations at that time wanted very much to talk. But we wanted to talk to him first. By various stratagems we got through the Japanese lines, and after about ten days of travel through the countryside, we found Ma. He greeted us as delegates from the League of Nations. We constantly denied this, stating that we were only newspaper correspondents trying to get a story. But since my colleague was carrying a card which identified him as from Geneva, Switzerland, we were not believed.

From my arrival until the outbreak of World War II, Shanghai was the news capital of China. That is where the international news agencies had their offices and where the correspondents of leading foreign newspapers were based. Virtually all news out of China was funneled through Shanghai. The only other news centers of consequence were Peking, Nanking, and (later) Chungking. With its cosmopolitan population and its sinful reputation, Shanghai was an interesting place to be stationed. Life was comfortable, news plentiful, and communications good. The town had no fewer than four English-language daily newspapers, along with an array of Chinese publications to be watched closely for hot tips from back-country correspondents. Nanking, then the capital, was only an overnight train trip. This situation began to change in the late 1930s with the Japanese invasion of central China and the transfer of the Chinese government from Nanking to Chungking, a thousand miles farther up the Yangtze. Many of the Shanghai news colony found it advisable to follow.

Shanghai drew another young adventurer and Depression refugee, Tillman Durdin, who by the mid-1940s was the New York Times's *premier correspondent in China.*

I arrived like many others, as an adventurer, a hippie of an earlier era. I was working on a newspaper in Houston, Texas, and decided that I had to see the world, but I had no money. So I got myself a job as a workaway on an American ship and scrubbed decks and cleaned winches for a couple of months, crossing through the Panama Canal up the West Coast and across the Pacific to Japan where I applied for a job on the *Japan Advertiser.* There was no opening. So I continued on to Shanghai and went ashore and found that I could get a job on the *Shanghai Evening Post and Mercury.* I gladly loaded my luggage over the side into a sampan one night, went ashore, never to return to the good ship *Scottsburg,* and started a career in China journalism. Harold Isaacs and I worked on the *Shanghai Evening Post.* I became the real estate editor. Shanghai was booming. While people in the United States were standing in bread lines, we in Shanghai were prospering.

I had an eight-page real estate section. Harold worked as a reporter. At one stage we decided that we weren't getting enough money and we could force the *Shanghai Evening Post* to the wall if we went on strike. We quit and tried to play *jai alai* for a living for a while. That didn't work, and surprisingly enough the *Evening Post* went right ahead without us. Fortunately at that time Chinese interests took over the *China Press,* which had been owned by a prominent Jewish family in Shanghai up to then and had become a poor newspaper. Hal and I applied for a job on this paper. Hollington Tong, who had been put in charge, said, "Yes, I'll hire both of you. I need a city editor and one of you can be city editor one week, and the other one the next week." We managed for quite a while, much to the bewilderment of the staff. Eventually Harold decided it wasn't working well. Anyway, he developed larger interests. He took a vacation, went up the Yangtze River, saw the misery of China, and decided to get more actively engaged in Chinese political affairs. He established his own publication, *The China Forum.* I was left with the *China Press,* and Hollington Tong made me managing editor, in which job I had also to do a little reporting. I was the night news editor, made up the paper, went home at two o'clock every morning and started work at ten the next day. I began to be a fill-in man for the *New York Times,* since Hallett Abend needed somebody to file whenever he left Shanghai for the interior. Having done this for several years, when the Japanese war broke out in

1937, I was asked by the *Times* to join its staff. They needed someone quickly. Jack Belden and I hired an automobile and drove through the Japanese lines to Nanking, where I took up my duties. Jack served as a UP correspondent.

Jack Belden, war correspondent and author of several insightful books on China, was also a product of the Depression. Belden recalled his arrival in China in a post-conference interview.

I had just gotten out of college (Colgate) in 1933, during the Depression, and couldn't get a job. So I went to sea. I decided to jump ship in Hamburg, Germany, but was talked out of it by a prostitute I met. She said I wouldn't live long if I stayed there. So I went back and finally wound up in Hong Kong, where I did jump ship on Armistice Day 1933, with a total of ten cents in my pockets. I needed a place to lie down for the night, so I started climbing a hill above the city looking for a nice grassy spot. After walking for awhile I came to a wall, climbed over it in the darkness and found a bit of clear space on the other side, where I went to sleep. When I woke up in the morning, I saw that I had fallen asleep right beside an open reservoir. I was lucky I hadn't rolled off into it and drowned. I eventually got to Shanghai where I made some money playing *jai alai* and gambling.

During the next several years I traveled between Shanghai and Peking and began learning the Chinese language. I spent some time working for the *Shanghai Evening Post and Mercury* and made some extra money by making language cards and teaching Chinese to foreigners. I was in Peking when the Japanese attacked [the Marco Polo Bridge] in 1937.

Unlike the others, Israel Epstein was raised in China. As a teenager he worked on various English-language dailies in the Peking-Tientsin area and later for the United Press. Epstein offered a caricature of US-China reporting before 1937:

The reporting was mainly about how what was happening in China affected foreigners. That was the main task. When I joined the UP in 1936 we were required to file stories like the following:

> Paul Price, Presbyterian missionary of Plymptonville, Pa., narrowly escaped death when a stray bullet ripped the drapes of the east window of his house in Changchow, China, during a shoot-out between Chinese warlord troops last night. His sister Sara lives at 77 Spruce St., Plymptonville.
>
> The American flag was flying over the house. U.S. Consul Sheamas Sheean in Shanghai says he will protest and demand compensation for the drapes as soon as it is clear which side fired the shot, which isn't yet known. U.S. Navy is investigating.
>
> Seven Chinese soldiers and 700 civilians were reported killed in the fray, in which most of Changchow was burned to the ground. . . .

In that order of paragraphs and of importance. Then you waited for the weekly cabled round-up from New York, hoping it would not say:

> Rocks (the AP) said the bullet also nicked Price's portico and that his brother Bill lives in Buffalo. Sister Sara silent, unquotable. But Bill gave Rocks grand quote, "Paul's scared of nothing at all since he got the call." We goofed. Don't do it again.

This was a stiff rebuke. Too many of them, and you were fired. The example is fictitious, but every old UP writer will recognize it as true in essence.

My own first boss in the UP, in Tientsin, taught me

the priorities. When our colleague in Peking [Mac Fisher] was two hours late reporting another firefight in that city, he said for my instruction, "You know why he was behind. Instead of cabling as soon as he heard, the horse's ass had to go and see for himself."

Only after the Sino-Japanese war broke out in 1937 did Chinese events begin to move into first place over the parish pump.

The nature of reporting in China changed dramatically when the Japanese opened fire at the Marco Polo Bridge in 1937 and ushered in an eight-year war between China and Japan. As the capital of China moved from Nanking to Hankow and finally to Chungking, China reporting became more serious and important. Work conditions changed, and so did the product. Most agree that the most open period came early, in 1938, when the seat of government was Hankow.

3 | Romantic Hankow, 1938

Within a half-year of the declaration of war after the Marco Polo Bridge Incident of July 7, 1937, Peking, Shanghai, and Nanking fell to the Japanese. The Nationalists retreated to Hankow, in the plains of central China. Hankow was and is part of a tri-city industrial complex known as Wuhan that straddles the Yangtze River midway down its long meandering course from the Himalayas to the sea. Helped in part by a major victory at Taierhchuang in April 1938, the Chinese were able to hold on to Hankow until October 1938. Thus for about ten months Hankow became the wartime capital of a new China in which the Communists and the Kuomintang formed a united front. Spirits were high, and for the first time in a decade there was a semblance of unity. In retrospect, this was the most romantic period of China's wartime experience, and it generated a mood of optimism and idealism that was tempered only partially by the harsh realities of war.

Out of desperation, China seemed to be coming together politically and militarily. There was a sense of unified purpose and determination that had not been seen since the early 1920s. Foreign journalists enjoyed the freest atmosphere of any Chinese capital before or since.

Moreover, Hankow had international glamour. In 1938 it was catapulted to center stage in worldwide press attention because of Franco's victory in Spain. As historian Charles Hayford put it:

While it lasted, Hankow became a world center for the democratic struggle against fascism, and became almost a tourist stop-off for writers and demi-diplomats who swooped through to visit the front.

Tillman Durdin reminisced about Hankow at the conference. He began by discussing the "polyglot" nature of the press corps in China during the 1930s and 1940s—meaning that it comprised a core of professionals surrounded by all sorts of part-timers, stringers, and political advocates. By advocacy is meant a political commitment to the victory of either the revolution or counter-revolution in China and elsewhere. In later years it was usually coupled with strong opinions about American involvement in China and the forms it should take.

At Hankow we had a large number of people who had had some experience of the Spanish Civil War and who had been in Moscow. They brought with them very worldly political points of view. They felt at home in China because she, too, was fighting a just war like the one they had been pushing, observing, and covering in Spain on the Republican side. They were also great believers in the Russian Revolution. So at Hankow, with their presence, we had become part of the world scene.

This was the romantic period of Chinese resistance to the Japanese. It was also the height of the united front. Chou En-lai was in Hankow, and there seemed to be unity between the Communists and the Kuomintang about fighting the Japanese. The unity tremendously impressed us. Although the Chinese were losing steadily after some very tough battles, their sense of unity as a people seemed to hold. We tried to report this in whatever we wrote.

We correspondents operated in relative freedom. There was censorship, usually about battlefield statistics, but by and large we were able to get the story out. Occasionally we were able to get into the field with the Chinese troops and see what was going on. Generally, we relied on Jack Belden and Joseph Stilwell, who collaborated in keeping track of where the Chinese armies were and what they were doing. Jack and Stilwell would plunge off into the hinterland and come back with information about the situation at the front, all of which was made available to us.

Very pervasive at Hankow was close collaboration and friendship between correspondents and American officials. I have mentioned Stilwell, but John Davies was also in the consulate at the time. He and others were eager to get all the information we had and vice versa. There was nothing of the confrontational and mutually suspicious approach to one another that has characterized press-government relations in more recent years. At that time we felt that we were all in this together and in the right. China, after all, was being invaded and brutalized by the Japanese, and we had deep sympathy for the Chinese side. This created a spirit of mutual sympathy and cooperation among us.

The cosmopolitan nature of the foreign press corps was extraordinary. There were quite a few Europeans drifting in and out, some with experience in Spain and others in Moscow. Anna Louise Strong and Agnes Smedley were two colorful figures who brought this kind of international world view to Hankow. Freda Utley was another. Once an

English Communist, she brought the Moscow view in reverse. She had turned categorically anti-Communist by this time, counterbalancing the united frontists who still thought the Russian Revolution was inspiring. Indeed, reporting on what the Russians were doing in China was a sensitive subject, about which the Chinese government was not eager to have publicity. We saw huge Russian aircraft flying from time to time over Hankow and occasionally spotted a Russian in the city, but it was difficult to find out much about Russian aid or activity. Equally difficult to follow was the German Military Advisory Group. There was the ever present Captain Walther Stennes, who was a sort of front man for the group and advisor to Chiang Kai-shek. He was very affable and likable but we never found out much about him.

Of special interest in retrospect was the presence of Chou En-lai and his Communist delegation, who were very accessible. Chou held press conferences for correspondents from time to time. His influence and that of his delegation were not as great as later in the Chungking days, but they were still significant. Also he was more a part of the government than he was later, and this had an inhibiting effect. Viewing himself as a kind of government spokesman, Chou tried not to reveal more than Hollington Tong or one of the Kuomintang officials would reveal. Later, in the Chungking days, the breach was such that Chou would gladly fill correspondents in on all the dirt they wanted about the doings of Chiang's circle and the Kuomintang government in general.

As Durdin suggests, the range of journalistic personalities in Hankow was extraordinary. Yet a remarkable camaraderie or esprit de corps *prevailed. This collegiality* was especially noticed and appreciated by those who were closer to the fringe of American journalism, or further from the establishment, than Durdin. One such figure was Agnes Smedley, for whom Hankow was a social oasis.

Smedley was an advocate journalist in quite a different tradition from Henry Luce. She saw the Communists as the key to China's future and had been writing since 1929 about their struggle in the countryside in clear, simple, driving prose for the international left-of-center press. She arrived in Hankow in January 1938, fresh from a year in the northwest with the Communist-led Eighth Route guerrilla army, including a stay in the mountain citadel of Yenan.

Oddly enough, she too was from Missouri—the product of a dirt-poor tenant farm, not a school of journalism. Later, in turn-of-the-century Western mining towns, she learned to ride, shoot, and write. Politically she evolved into an anarchist of the old IWW type and was arrested in New York for work with the Indian nationalist movement in 1919. Once out of jail, she worked on the socialist daily The Call. During the 1920s Smedley lived in Germany, visited Moscow, and befriended Emma Goldman. She came to China in 1929 to fight imperialism, see the revolution, and write for the Frankfurter Zeitung. She soon felt in her gut that rural China was where the real story was. Thus, by 1938, with two China books under her belt, she had shifted her focus to the Communist-led guerrilla resistance to the Japanese in North China. Hankow put her back in touch with the world at large, and she was slightly overwhelmed. Just after the fall of Hankow, she wrote to Freda Utley, one of the few women in the group:

The last days of Hankow still remain in my mind as rare, unusual days from the psychological and human viewpoint. I still think of Shaw's *Heartbreak House* when I recall them. As you remarked at the time, no person on earth is more charming than the American journalist abroad, particularly the cultured serious-minded ones. But I wonder what it would be like were I to meet those same men on the streets of Chicago. Gone the Magic![1]

At about the same time, Smedley wrote a letter addressed simply to the Hankow "Gang." In it she fantasized about writing a play in which the lead characters would be the Hankow fraternity of journalists and American government officials. Lovingly, she portrayed each of them:

I shall one day try to weave you all into a drama—John [Davies, American consular official], you with your white bowls filled with lovely flowers, with Beethoven's Fifth Symphony in the background. And, I suspect, behind your immaculate life, many dark thoughts and dreams. You are so much a part of this bourgeois, cultured civilization of the present you do not even know other ways of life. Very well, with all that you shall be a leading character in my play. Then there is Evans [Carlson, office of the US naval attaché]—where is he? Long and lanky and lovable, he shall be the man unconsciously reaching for the stars—but never touching them I fear. Yet that striving, alone, makes life worthwhile. He shall be the element of tragedy in my play. And you Walter [Bosshard, Swiss journalist], I have to try and recall your speech at Freda's and Carlson's last farewell party. I shall reproduce that, but make all readers love you and long to pat your head. George [Hogg] I shall use as a background because his voice is suitable for sound effects and because he is young and unformed (save physically); and because he is a vigorous opposite of John. Till [Durdin] shall be the psychological case, reticent, fearful of himself as a man, yet trembling a bit at times before the harsh reality of his psychological problems. Arch [Steele] the disciplined—perhaps all too disciplined—looking with amused eyes on the passing scene. Yet at times of which I know so little—deeply moved by joy and sorrow. I shall give him seven wives and one child, but they shall be but the comedy element in the offing, while the real Arch shall be tousled and beaten down at times. Mac [Fisher] of many hidden problems—kind and generous but lovable, and something more, though I have not yet fathomed it. Freda [Utley] shall be the flame, uncontrolled and forever attracting all, instinctively and unconsciously. Mayell [Eric, newsreel photographer] I never understood; and Mr. Josselyn [American consul general] and Col. Stilwell who did not quite make the gang and never wanted to. And above all [there is] Jack Belden. Jack can be drawn down into chaos or led into a purposeful life, but not in China—at least not the way he is going.[2]

Jack Belden was one of the most remarkable figures of the war years and as a war correspondent probably the best of the bunch, as acknowledged earlier by Durdin. Belden jumped directly into the field, working closely with Col. Joseph Stilwell as a military reporter.

At the conference Charles Hayford discussed Belden and the significance of his work at length. Suffice it to say that Belden was a gifted journalist writing about war in depth with rare poetical insight. But he was also a difficult, elusive, and alcoholic figure. Today his work is amongst the most enduring of the period. And earlier his

bravery and insight inspired respect from colleagues—
and for some, like Hugh Deane and Israel Epstein, Belden
assumed the role of teacher.

Today Belden lives in angry exile in Paris. Black-
listed by McCarthyism and silent for decades, his vision
and inimitable style remain unclouded, as in this pas-
sage from a letter of protest to the conference organizers
about the application of the term advocacy journalism *to*
some of his writings:

The trouble with most journalists, reporters, diplomats or otherwise is they have no poetry in their souls.
Many historians have acknowledged that Shakespeare's
Julius Caesar shows a better and more succinct and powerful understanding of the fall of the Roman Empire than a
batch of historic tomes. His *Troilus and Cressida* might
have been written about why the Vietnam war went on.
When Nixon sent US troops into Cambodia he said America could not be a "pitiful giant." Some four hundred years
ago in *Measure for Measure,* Isabella told Angelo, "O it is
excellent to have a giant's strength, but tyrannous to use it
like a giant. . . . Man proud man dressed in little brief authority plays such tricks before high heaven, etc." And
you, dressed in the brief authority of a Center for Asian
Studies, presume to tag me (in a bad sense) with the term
advocacy journalist. Bah! Give me an ounce of civet to
sweeten my imagination.

American journalists are taught objectivity. That's all
fine, quote this leader and that leader, etc. But it often
leads to a gross error and that is the interplay of the sub-
jective and the objective. "Look into thy heart and write,"
said Sidney. That is what journalists too often do not do or
are scared to do. In the time of falling nations what ordi-

nary people feel has an effect on events they do not have in quieter times. Into whose poor people's hearts do you and your war reporters look? As for my own reporting of facts—and I made a distinction between reporting and writing—if you will go to the United States Army, I am sure you will find military maps on the Shanghai war of 1937 there which I objectively gathered and gave to Stilwell. Or if you will look in OSS files. In 1940 I gathered some 50,000 words (facts, not writing) on Japanese and Chinese terror organizations in Shanghai, a great deal from the police. When the Japs captured Shanghai (I was not there) these papers were in a safe. They were thrown in a furnace and burned. Wild Bill Donovan somehow— God knows how—heard about it and one of his agents came to see me in a hospital when I was wounded. I gave them a copy of the material, at least on the Japanese, on Mitsui and Mitsubishi who ran the drug trade and facts on murders. They did not think I was an advocate, they have some sense of my objective facts.

Enough! I have indulged myself in a long-winded diatribe. But I refuse to be hung for what I am not. Since your conference is in some sense on war, I close with a poem by Wordsworth. If, as Henri IV said, Paris is worth a mass, then war is worth a sonnet.

> The power of Armies is a visible thing
> Formal and circumscribed in time and space;
> But who the limits of that power shall trace
> Which a brave People into light can bring
> Or hide, at will, for freedom combating
> By just revenge inflamed? No foot may chase,
> No eye can follow, to a fatal place
> That power, that spirit, whether on the wing
> Like the strong wind, or sleeping like the wind
> Within its awful caves.—From year to year
> Springs this indigenous produce far and near;

No craft this subtle element can bind,
Rising like water from the soil, to find
In every nook a lip that it may cheer.

Hankow then was a unique, heady experience for the American journalist. Extraordinary camaraderie and romance filled the air. The atmosphere was free, partly because the united front between Chiang Kai-shek and the Communists was at its most cordial. Moreover, the writing to be done from Hankow was relatively simple—reporting on the struggle of the united, heroic Chinese versus the villainous Japanese. In reaction to the tension, drama, and hopelessness of the situation, the correspondents responded with an almost macabre gaiety. Symbolic of the Hankow spirit among journalists was the formation during the summer of 1938 of the Last Ditchers Club. The group assembled regularly with much rhetorical flourish for farewell dinners to see off "deserters." The idea was to see who would hold out in Hankow the longest. One such dinner was staged as a trial of the guests of honor. The charges illustrate beautifully the Hankow spirit of 1938, and the need for comic relief from the bombs, corpses, and wounded.

CHARGE

IN THE SUPREME COURT of the Hankow Last Ditchers Corps within and for the District of East Asia, in the first Judicial Circuit, in the year of our Lord one thousand nine hundred and thirty-eight.

THE GRAND JURORS of the Hankow Last Ditchers Corps, duly empaneled, sworn and charged with inquiring in and for the said district, upon their oaths and affirmations, present that Freda Clayfoot Utley and Evans Voice-in-the-Wilderness Carlson during, to wit, the last days of September in the year of our Lord 1000 900 & 38 in the Lutheran Mission Home and Rosie's Dine, Dance and Romance Restaurant in the district aforesaid and within the jurisdiction of this court, did, then, and there, in contravention to the Corps line, knowingly and with force of arms connive to commit—desertion, contrary to the form of the statute in such case made and provided, and against the peace, dialectics and dignity of the Hankow Last Ditchers Corps.

And the Grand Jurors aforesaid, upon their oaths and affirmations aforesaid, do further present that the defendants, on, to wit, the last days of September, of the year of our Lord, etc., in the L.M.H. and R.D.D.R.R., in the district aforesaid, and within the jurisdiction of this court, through their connivance to commit desertion,

2nd Specification	Wreck and create diversion of the defense plans of the Hankow Last Ditchers Corps;
3rd Specification	Sabotage the economic warp and woof;
4th Specification	Sap, gut and scuttle Corps morale; contrary to the form of the statutes in such case made and provided, and against the peace, dialectics and dignity of the Hankow Last Ditchers Corps.

A. T. Steele
Presiding Judge

Note: Witnesses testify on only second, third and fourth counts. First count (desertion) will be stated by the prosecutor to be self-evident as defendants will be led during the course of the meal to state that they cannot join the Corps as they intend to depart.[3]

Chungking: A
Different Time and
A Different Place

When the Japanese army captured Hankow in October 1938, Chiang Kai-shek moved the seat of Chinese government to Chungking, a city in the remote southwestern province of Szechwan. For the next seven years, until their abrupt surrender in 1945, the Japanese occupied communication routes and major cities in the rest of China. Principally in rural north China, the Communists developed anti-Japanese guerrilla bases, governing some ninety million people by 1945. Chiang for the most part waited out the war in Chungking, with the international press and diplomatic corps in attendance.

At Chungking, the ranks of American correspondents were expanded and reporting methods changed considerably, especially after the bombing of Pearl Harbor. Living and working conditions were more primitive than they had been in Shanghai or Hankow. Arch Steele recaptured the mood of the initial Chungking years.

For the newsmen the move to Chungking was no cause for rejoicing. Situated on a steep, rocky tongue at the confluence of the Yangtze and Chialing rivers, China's wartime capital did indeed boast a setting of impressive natural beauty. Its other attributes, however, were mostly negative. During the long wet season, the natural beauty was largely obscured for weeks on end by soggy, low-hanging clouds. And clear weather, when it came, brought something worse—wave upon wave of Japanese planes, dropping their bombs indiscriminately over the congested landscape. On those occasions, most of the population took to the tunnels that pockmarked Chungking's hillsides and sat miserably in the dank shelters until the all-clear sounded. Nightlife in Chungking was almost non-existent except for the rats roaming the streets and sitting saucily on the great stone stairways leading down to the river's edge. Most of the decent housing in town had already been requisitioned for government officials and diplomatic personnel by the time the correspondents arrived, and we were assigned accommodations in a jerry-built government structure christened the Press Hostel. It served our basic needs.

Ironically, Pearl Harbor brought some improvement in our overall situation. All of a sudden Japan and the United States were at war, and beleaguered China had a powerful ally. Japanese bombers were too busy elsewhere to bother any more with Chungking. American military personnel began arriving to discuss ways of stepping up the movement of supplies into the blockaded country. But China was at the far end of the world's supply line and had a low priority on the Allies' shopping list, so the effect on the war's outcome of all the effort that ensued was probably negligible.

Principal news sources in Chungking included the government information office, presided over by Hollington Tong, and the Chinese Communist liaison office, where correspondents were often able to talk with Chou En-lai or one of his assistants. Despite the cease-fire that was supposed to exist between the Nationalist and Communist forces, continuous jockeying for position led to serious armed clashes. Indeed, there were many times when the two camps seemed more interested in fighting each other than in fighting the Japanese. This was a source of despair to people like General Stilwell, who were interested only in getting on with the war. Stilwell was a favorite with the correspondents because of his down-to-earth approach to all subjects and his outspoken contempt for stupidity at all levels. He was in some ways a tragic figure. Interviews with Chiang Kai-shek or Madame Chiang, on the other hand, were usually arranged for correspondents through Hollington Tong, a man so in awe of his boss that I have seen him tremble visibly in the Gimo's presence.

Chungking had many facets. Annalee Jacoby [Fadiman] was new to China. Fresh out of Stanford and two years of writing movie scripts for MGM, she contrasted the "heroic" atmosphere of 1941 with the sordid Chungking of 1944.

The Nationalists were living in mud and bamboo shacks. They were the most heroic, intelligent people. They were making do with nothing. Living conditions were terrible, the city was filled with rats, the food was dreadful, bomb craters everywhere. Everything was slimy, cold, wet, and mildewed. In the summer, the humidity was high and bugs flourished. There were spiders four inches across on the walls of your room. The press hostel had just been bombed. When they rebuilt it, it was just one storey, built of bamboo and mud with whitewash on the outside and oiled paper for windows, a wooden floor. All the water had to be carried up from the Yangtze River in wooden buckets and we had one little tin basin of water a day to bathe in, that's all. The rats chewed our boots and through the telephone wires at night. They ate our soap. But though it was most uncomfortable physically, it was absolutely inspiring mentally. It was a great year!

By 1944 the situation had changed almost completely. Inflation had increased so that no one could afford to be honest any more, and all our old idealistic friends from 1941 had to do rather unsavory things in order to stay alive and feed their children.

Chiang Kai-shek was still appeasing warlords, still having to print so much paper money that it was worthless. The country was going down the drain of inflation. Chiang's troops were starving. Some didn't even have straw sandals to go into battle. Censorship was terrible, and by then there was something to conceal. We were working first through the Chinese censor, who couldn't let you say anything against his government and didn't want you to say anything that might hurt the feelings of the Americans. Then what was left of the dispatch—if anything—had to be taken up to the American military censor who wouldn't let you say anything that might hurt our allies' feelings and, of course, wouldn't let you say anything about mistakes the American military was making in the war. So almost not a word got back to this country for over two years.

Wartime Chungking could be dangerous. Peggy Durdin told of one moonlit night when Edgar Snow was a house guest of the Durdins. After waiting a while for the Japanese to begin bombing the city (they only attacked on bright nights), they decided to retire.

We all got into bed, and then the siren went off. It was law in Chungking that you had to go to the air-raid shelter. Soldiers could shoot you if you didn't. Ed—separated from us by a thin wall of bamboo with some mud slapped on it—and Till lay in bed. But I was up, anxious to get to the shelter. I'm a physical coward.

I kept saying, "Get the hell out of bed!" and Ed said to Till, "How many houses do you think are in Chungking?"

"I don't know, a couple million. Why?"

"I was just thinking about the law of probability."

Till said, "That's fascinating!"

Ed said, "How many flights of Japanese planes? How many planes in each flight? Multiply that by the bomb load and multiply that by the number of houses in Chungking, and the chance of our house getting bombed is one in trillions."

All this time, I'm saying, "Just listen, get the hell out of bed!" So, sullenly, they got out of bed.

We all went to the shelter, and after five hours spent standing around complaining about the pointlessness and inconvenience of the trip, we returned to find our home had been leveled by a bomb blast. There was no wall, no house. We stood there. Till said nothing, but Ed turned around to me, put his arm around my shoulders, and said, "Peggy, I take back the whole goddamn law of probability."

That was one of the best things that ever happened to me. Of course, we lost everything in the house except one bottle of gin and a pair of Ed's underpants out on a bush. It taught me I didn't give a damn about anything except people.

How numerous on the China scene were women reporters like Peggy Durdin during the Chungking period? Steve MacKinnon noted that—at least relative to other parts of the world—there seem to have been a considerable number of American women in China in the 1930s, such as Agnes Smedley, Freda Utley, and Anna Louise Strong. John Service offered a possible explanation.

I think it's a fact that of the American missionaries who went to China, 60 percent were women. And I think that we may find some correlation between the fact that many American women went to China as missionaries and the fact that they were in such numbers in the press corps. One reason probably was a difficulty in getting satisfying substantial jobs at home, but the other one was the fact that a revolution, a social revolution, was going on in China in which women's rights, changes in women's life, and so on were a very important part. I think that these factors helped to draw women there and that most of the women we see there were committed to these interests. People like Agnes Smedley and others.

Annalee Jacoby Fadiman took issue with the claim that women played a significant role during the Chungking years.

Regarding women correspondents, the War Department wouldn't let women go to China. I tried to get to Chungking in late 1940 as a correspondent, and the War Department refused permission. They finally let me in as a representative of United China Relief, which was the pet child of Henry Luce and David Selznick, the movie producer. I had been writing motion pictures at MGM for two years, and the War Department let me go under the guise of a United China Relief representative. Then in 1944 I went back. That time Henry Luce was able to get me in because, he said, I was the only one who had been there in 1941. Agnes Smedley, Freda Utley, Anna Louise

Strong, Peggy Durdin, Shelly Mydans, Betty Graham, all of them were there before I arrived, and many came after, but the War Department prevented our coming during the war years, which was the only time I knew.

Mary Sullivan backed up Annalee's statements.

I was in China from 1946 to 1950, with the US Information Service, not as a correspondent, and then worked for the *China Weekly Review* after that. Natalie Hankemeyer was there with the World Church Religious News Service. Dorothy Borg, who will speak for herself, was there with the Institute of Pacific Relations. Betty Graham was in and out. The other ones were there because they were with their husbands, who were correspondents—not that they themselves were not qualified correspondents—I can mention Lee Martin, who was there with Pepper Martin, *U.S. News and World Report;* Ann Doyle, who was there with Bob Doyle from Time-Life; and Lynn Landman, who was there with her husband for the Overseas News Agency; and, of course, Peggy Durdin.

Henry Lieberman expanded on this theme.

One of the things that we forget, I think, is that women in journalism in the United States were not much in evidence until recent years. One of the things that struck me (I don't know whether it's true, these are just impressions) is that women writers in China were book writers for the most part. Anna Louise Strong and Agnes Smedley had connections with outfits like the North American Newspaper Alliance, which was not one of your major news organizations, but they were essentially writers of books.

There were exceptions, such as Peggy Durdin, who later became a correspondent for *Newsweek* in India.

I didn't get out to China until late 1944, so I don't have firsthand knowledge before that time. The first woman correspondent I ran into who did the kind of work that the staff reporters did, aside from Annalee, was Charlotte Ebener, who worked for International News Service (INS). She got to China because she offered to pay her own expenses [actually paid by the International Red Cross— ed.], and INS paid her salary. I remember late in the war, there was a woman correspondent out there for *Vogue Magazine*, Mary Jane Kempner. She was dealing with women's fashions and I found it very hard to figure out why. But my main point is that women journalists were in short supply in the United States until recent years, and that is conceivably one reason why there were so few women reporters in China. To be sure, the War Department frowned on their going to China, but I'm sure that if there had been a large number of women journalists in the United States and that if the atmosphere then had been what it is now, they somehow would have found a way to get to China or any other place.

Another feature that separated Chungking from Shanghai and Hankow was the presence of two distinguishable groups of journalists. Although some veteran correspondents, such as J. B. Powell and Randall Gould, remained in Shanghai, most made the trek to Chungking, where they were joined by a younger generation of new arrivals. Albert Ravenholt was one of them.

I'm basically a farm boy. I was working at the New York World's Fair in 1939 when the war started in Europe, and I decided I did not want to go back to college. I didn't want to miss the war, so, like Till Durdin, I shipped at sea and took off for China. (Till, I think, shipped on deck, and I was the chief cook on the ship. I won't guarantee what the food was like.) Anyway, I settled down in Shanghai to study Chinese and Russian and worked on a radio station there. In June of 1941 Walter Briggs and I smuggled our way through the Japanese lines into the interior of China. Nobody was interested in news of the interior then, so I got a job with the International Red Cross supervising distribution of medical supplies throughout the interior. I traveled to northwest China and southeast China. After Pearl Harbor, the United Press became more interested in hiring young fellows, and I was hired to cover a number of the fronts in China, India, and Burma. I was bureau chief in India and Burma when Peggy Durdin introduced me to my wife. That was at the end of the war in China, Walt Rundle having gone home.

Another new face on the scene was Hugh Deane, who first visited China as an exchange student to Lingnan University from Harvard in 1936. He returned in 1940 as a string correspondent for the Christian Science Monitor *and the* Springfield (Massachusetts) Union and Republican.

In Shanghai I called on the *Monitor's* chief correspondent, Randall Gould. He had been threatened by the Japanese, and the entrance to his house was protected by sandbags. Stopping over in Hong Kong I saw Guenther Stein, who also contributed to the *Monitor*, and he gave me a note to Ch'en Han-sheng (Chen Han-sen), author of *Landlord and Peasant in China* and other influential studies of the Chinese countryside. I saw Ch'en on the fly, because I had a date to interview Eugene Chen, who was foreign minister in the Hankow government. Ch'en Han-sheng decided to give me a very quick education on China so that I could perform properly as a correspondent. "What's the most important thing about China?" he asked me. I mumbled and finally said, "Well, most of the people are poor." "That's not it," he said. "The most important single thing about China is that politics and economics are the same thing. If you keep that in mind, you'll do well."

Accompanied by my bride, I went to Chungking the hard way, through Haiphong and Hanoi and north through Kwangsi and Kweichow. In Chungking I was happy to have as companions two others who had gone to Lingnan University, Melville Jacoby, a *Time* correspondent, and Betty Graham, who was then working for Hollington Tong and was later a partisan of the Chinese Revolution. She was with the New Fourth Army in Shantung during the Civil War. Both died young, tragically.

Soon after I reached Chungking, I lucked into an interview with Yeh Ting, commander of the New Fourth Army. He was living disconsolately in a cheap hotel, frustrated in his effort to extract supplies for his army from the Ministry of Defense. I fired off a long story to the *Monitor* and got it back in print rewritten by Gordon Walker, later the *Monitor* correspondent in Tokyo. I learned how to write a news story by carefully studying the rewrites the *Monitor* sent me.

I learned a great deal from Jack Belden. He had come up from Shanghai having read Trotsky's *The Revolution Betrayed*, from which he had drawn a series of twenty-eight or thirty questions to ask about the internal situation in Kuomintang China. He wasn't a Trotskyite. He just used Trotsky's works to get some basic knowledge about the nature of revolution. Belden sensed that I didn't know very much. He took me in hand, and I went with him to a lot of interviews. He told me things and pointed me in the right direction. I think of him as my teacher.

And I must say Agnes Smedley contributed to my education, too. I know she could be prickly, but when she got to Chungking from the guerrilla areas in Hupeh, not at all well, she let me interview her most of an afternoon. She didn't think of me as someone who could take the edge off her story but as someone who could get important information out. I think the interview took place in the Butterfield & Swire house on the South Bank.

The younger correspondents seemed to mix well and learn from the more seasoned journalists, like James White, Durdin, Steele, and Belden. Many of the newcomers came as employees of the United States Office of War Information (OWI), set up by the veteran journalist and former UP bureau chief, Mac Fisher. Christopher Rand was a member of this "new breed." His biographer, son Peter, recalled:

I want to talk about some people who, I believe, set a new journalistic standard in China as the direct result of the involvement of the United States in China in the war against Japan. These are the young men who came out with the US Office of War Information. The OWI in China was charged, theoretically anyway, with the task of informing the Chinese people about the United States' war effort. The young recruits were people who either had China backgrounds or had backgrounds in journalism. Mac Fisher, who was the head of OWI in China, wanted men working under him who had grown up on a farm, because he believed that people who grew up on a farm knew how to fix almost anything if they had to, and did not stop working at five o'clock in the afternoon. This seemed to have been particularly true of these men. When they did fix something, they made it work right. The men who came out were offbeat by temperament. They did not think of themselves as strictly journalists. They thought of themselves as writers, and some of them had already published books, although they were quite young. Graham Peck, who was in China when he joined the OWI, was the author of *Through China's Wall*, a superb travel account of China ending with a description of the Japanese occupation of Peking in 1937, in which he was very much involved. Jim Burke, the son of a missionary, wrote a biography of his father called *My Father in China*, which is fresh reading today. It's useful to us because it contains an intimate account of the rise of the Soongs to national prominence. These people were precocious and somewhat off the beaten track.

Christopher Rand also thought of himself as a writer. In the late 1930s he had helped to found a magazine in San Francisco called *The Coast*, modeled loosely on *The New Yorker*. It was a combination of nonfiction and short fiction which included among its regular contributors John Steinbeck and William Saroyan. Rand, when he worked for *The Coast*, was both an editor and a writer for the magazine. He subsequently worked for the *San Francisco Chronicle*.

Now OWI provided these men with an unusual opportunity to become China specialists. It gave them, first of all, a chance to travel around China, particularly around southeast China, around Chungking-held China, which was not that easy to do. They were civilians in the war effort, and they were very fortunate, as civilians, to be able to get around and see the countryside. They were also encouraged to learn rudimentary Chinese, and they were paid to take language lessons. Rand, for example, took Chinese lessons every day while he was in China.

Christopher Rand was in Fukien Province for over a year. He ran a listening post behind Japanese lines and supervised a crew of twenty Chinese and three Americans. His job was really twofold. First, he distributed US news to about 141 Chinese regional newspapers in the four provinces under his control. The other thing he did, and this was somewhat unofficial, was to send reports to military intelligence in Chungking. He also wrote reports, which he sent along to the Chungking office and which were forwarded, of course, to Washington. These reports are good examples of hard news, hard information, detailed reporting about provincial China. They dealt, for example, with relations between the KMT and local governments, the youth corps, and data on Chinese armies and secret societies. The main problem that he tackled in these reports was doping out the truth behind Chungking news falsification. This was something that he and his colleagues in OWI were particularly alert to and which they carried with them into their careers as journalists reporting on the Chinese Civil War after World War II ended.

Also, as a result of their training and their experience in the business of information in China, they were very conscious of the importance of proof in reporting.

They saw how propaganda was used badly, how falsified information was sent out by Chungking to buoy up the Chinese people. They saw how putting a face on things boomeranged, and they were against it. This gave them an *esprit de corps*. They felt a great bond with one another and you could see this later in their letters during the Civil War. They kept in touch as best they could, wherever they were in China. When they visited the States, they wrote to their friends in China.

Rand was very close to Graham Peck and learned a great deal about China from him. Peck had a good grasp of the Chinese people and also of the situation in China. The difference between truth and propaganda was something that especially concerned him. Later he wrote about it in *Two Kinds of Time*, which Rand helped him edit. My father was also close to Bill Powell. At one point, Bill went off to Yunnan with Sylvia for a honeymoon, and my father ran the *China Weekly Review* for him even though he was also working for the *Herald Tribune* at the time, as one of their correspondents in China. Jim Burke was up in Peking with his family, and his friends would gather whenever they visited Peking.

Now Christopher Rand believed that the readers were intelligent but were not being well enough informed. This idea, which he shared with friends who had been to gether in OWI, increased their sense of purpose. He set about to do the best he could to inform, and the way he believed you educated the public was not to give them spot news. He believed that the common prejudice that spot news is the best kind of news "can be connected with American short vision and opportunism." In an article published in the *Nieman Report* (he was a Nieman fellow in 1948–49), entitled "Reporting in the Far East," he wrote: "One of the best aids we had in China was personal observation, which was done by riding through the country in buses, wandering in alleys, consorting with soldiers and workers, drinking with generals, sleeping in small hotels, and watching what the people did all the while. For fun and education there was nothing like it. Floating from province to province one learned where the peasants were in rags and where they were clothed, which troops were disciplined and which were oppressive, what the merchants were buying, what the students were saying and so on. One couldn't begin to learn these things by sitting at a desk."

I think he succeeded in getting through to his readership. He dictated his articles before they were typed up and sent. Reading them today you hear his voice coming through. He was usually able to prevail on his newspaper to let him go where he wanted to go and to write what he wanted to write. Because his articles were constructed in this way, they were hard to edit, and so they were given pretty much the space and the prominence that he wanted for them. His paper backed him up in controversy. They respected his writing. Furthermore, I think it must be said that he did not believe in taking a political position in his reporting. He really had a belief that one must be as detached from politics as one possibly could. He was something of a mystic all his life, something of a Buddhist and something of a Taoist, and he believed that a kind of Taoist detachment was very useful, particularly in reporting the news in China.

Rand was a romantic and basically a feature writer, in the tradition of Belden, Smedley, and others. Henry Lieberman, also an ex-OWI employee and spot news reporter, contrasted himself sharply with Chris Rand.

I don't fit the mold, I guess. I come from Missouri, like Millard, but on the basis of what I've learned about him, I don't think I'm anything like him. I also came to China under the auspices of the OWI, and I can't imagine two more different people than Chris Rand and myself. Nor did I know a darn thing about China before I got there. Truth to tell, I began in my childhood trying to become a specialist on France. I became fluent in the French language, learned an awful lot about French history, embarked in graduate school on writing a thesis on Léon Blum's *Front Populaire.* However, at the same time, as a journalist, I became interested in a subject that seemed to be fresh and important at the time: namely, how political propaganda came into the United States through news channels. I started studying the activities of agencies like the German Transocean Agency and Domei on the Japanese side. A friend of mine, Matt Gordon, was interested in that too and wrote a book called *News as a Weapon.* I was one of his many advisors. Eventually, when Elmer Davis became head of the OWI, Matt was given a mandate to set up an organization that would deal with this problem. He gathered together five people to help him. All of us had the title of chief news editor, which gave the Civil Service Commission an awful lot of problems. But when we had our first meeting, it turned out that although all five of us were knowledgeable about Europe, there was no Far Eastern expert in the group. This was not surprising. The technical problem we were dealing with required a certain amount of specialization. You couldn't automatically find someone who knew something about the Far East who was also interested in the particular subject we were concerned with. So, being the youngest in the group, I was assigned to become the Far Eastern expert. In a matter of a month, after picking the brains of all kinds of Far Eastern experts, I produced a master paper on the Japanese Greater East Asian Co-Prosperity Sphere. That immediately stamped me as the expert on the Far East. But, after a while, I found I couldn't get out of Washington, because I couldn't get a release to go anywhere else. As the war was drawing to an end, I got worried about missing a tremendous adventure. I felt that we were going through one of the most important things that I would ever encounter, and I wanted to get out somewhere and get involved in this war.

There were two men whom I started to propagandize: George Taylor and John Fairbank, who headed the OWI's Far Eastern Division. Somehow I succeeded in convincing one or both of them that I ought to be assigned to the Far East. Dick Watts left China at about that time, and I was given the task of replacing him. At least I was led to believe that I was being appointed to replace Dick. To make a long story short, I finally found myself headed for China toward the end of 1944. I got to Kunming, and two guys at the OWI tried to hijack me to write leaflets. I kept insisting, "No, I'm on my way to Chungking to be chief news editor." I finally succeeded in escaping their clutches and got to Chungking and assumed my job, but I certainly was no replacement for Dick Watts. I was the head of the OWI news operation in China, but only in theory. A lot of other people tried to get into that act, and often did.

One of the first things that struck me was that there was no reliable communication system American correspondents could use inside China. OWI—operating as the American Information Service (AIS) in China—two or three years earlier had established a short-wave radio telegraphic network to connect its half-dozen offices. The Army Public Relations Office (PRO) wanted to help accredited correspondents move their dispatches from outlying cities to the cable head. The US-China Armed Forces Agreement permitted the army to establish communications for its needs. Under this authority and building on the AIS experience, the efficient PRO short-wave network was developed, manned largely by Chinese operators and managed by AIS. It was known variously as the PRO network, the OWI network, or the USIS network. My part in it was probably my major contribution in China, small as it may have been.

So, in a nutshell, I got to China by accident. I picked up my Chinese by just being there and learning it the way a baby learns whatever language it speaks. I found this sufficiently helpful to be able to get around China, travel on buses, talk to peasants, and even talk to the Army people. Even where my own Chinese failed, I had enough of it to keep a loose check on interpreters, of whom I was always suspicious. I'm not basically interested in Taoism, Buddhism, and the like, although I have made stabs at trying to understand what all this is about. I was concerned with what makes this country tick. I suddenly found very quickly that it was almost impossible to find out what made it tick. Certainly, it was not a matter of going around taking polls among peasants. I found little correlation between what the peasants thought and what the Nationalist government was doing and what the Communists were doing. I found myself groping, searching for the guts of what was going on, always frustrated.

I remember something I read in going through the literature that was given me by the OWI when I took off for China. The passage advised the reader never to walk across the shafts of a rickshaw because the Chinese considered it bad luck. Well, once somewhere in the interior I just couldn't avoid stepping across the shaft of a rickshaw. I did so and found that nothing happened. So much for all I was told about China.

Another episode (Phil Potter will remember this) was an encounter with Chou En-lai that caused me to say at the time, "Today I am a man." I was very captivated by Chou, as so many other Americans were. At one time, however, a very important thing came up in connection with the Nationalist-Communist truce talks that were taking place through the good offices of the United States and General Marshall. Chiang Kai-shek's treaty with the Russians said that Nationalist troops were empowered to recover all Chinese territory that had been occupied by the Soviet army. On the other hand, Chou En-lai was arguing that two places in Inner Mongolia were held by "The People's Forces" and should not go to the Nationalist government. These places were Chihfeng in Jehol Province and Dolonor in Chahar Province.

Phil Potter and I had just had some trying times in Manchuria. We got back to Nanking, pretty exhausted, and found that the argument about Chihfeng and Dolonor was the hot story of the day. So we decided, right there on the spur of the moment, "Let's get up there to Inner Mongolia and see what's going on." We finally got to Chihfeng and found Soviet troops there and also the "People's Army," both in the same place.

I still have somewhere in my memorabilia a ten-ruble note signed by a Russian officer there. We had a hell of a time getting him to sign it, because he kept telling us that in the Soviet Union it's a crime to deface currency. By the time we got back to Nanking, unfortunately, the story had just about vanished. The world was concerned with some other crisis. But we did go around to see Chou En-lai. Our hero had lied to us, and we confronted him with, "How could you do this to us?" In effect, he shrugged his shoulders.

This was a terrible blow to me: my hero had misled us. In retrospect, I wasn't really angry at Chou, but it gave me a different insight into what was going on in China. They were playing hardball politics there, and I was a pawn. They looked upon me as somebody to be manipulated, and this put me on my guard.

Like Durdin, Lieberman alluded regularly to the cozy working relationship between representatives of the American press and American government civilian and military officials in China. When younger historians questioned the propriety of such a relationship, the issue quickly became a major one. The veterans (journalists and government officials alike) disclaimed any impropriety about the relationship. It was a completely natural and necessary interdependence, they argued, which should not be tainted by the confrontational hindsight and experiences of more recent years.

To begin with, the help of the Office of War Information (OWI) was pivotal in getting the journalists' job done during the Chungking years. John Fairbank elaborated.

I was in China in '45 and '46 as director of the American Information Service (AIS). That was the name of the rather extensive OWI operation in China. The brief point I would make is that reporting on China, which became reporting on the beginning of the Civil War, began as war reporting on the war against Japan. The important thing was to attain victory against the Japanese. In order to help that, the US Army and AIS developed a network of shortwave radio communications establishing telegraphic contact among the major cities. This was in effect an expansion of the radio network AIS had set up two or three years earlier to handle its own traffic. With its trained crew of Chinese radio operators and engineers, AIS managed the system. At the end of the war with Japan we continued on the wartime basis, providing radio communication in American channels between the different AIS offices and US consulates scattered over unoccupied, and then over reoccupied, China.

So the journalists, who had come to look at the Japanese war and found that a new kind of war was developing under their feet, had more than the US Air Force planes to move around in as war correspondents. They also had the facilities of a radio telegraph network to move their stories, which had begun as part of the war effort against Japan but continued in the postwar period. This is the context in which people were reporting.

In addition to sharing a communication system, diplomats and military personnel frequently shared information to an unprecedented degree. John Service, an American Foreign Service officer in China at the time, explained why this was necessary.

My experience in China was rather abruptly terminated early in 1945, so I can't speak from any knowledge after that period. But I was in Chungking from '41 to '45. You have to remember the special conditions holding in China: difficulty of travel; and as time went on, a completely censored press, completely controlled access to information, and very scanty information given out by official Kuomintang authorities. Trying to find out what was going on in China was a continual game. Everyone worked with everyone else on it. When any traveler came to town, anybody could talk to him, pass along information to him or pass on information gained from him. Interviews were generally spread around, although I don't know how much of this happened within the press corps.

Perhaps there was competition at some level, but I was working, for instance, in a very low capacity in Stilwell's headquarters. I was not known as Stilwell's political advisor—that was John Davies. In Chungking I was just a fifth wheel. I couldn't talk to somebody like T. V. Soong, but the Chungking correspondent for Time-Life, Teddy White, could. So Teddy, and many other correspondents, too, were willing to share very generously any information they had from any source. As long as the information that I was collecting was simply political information on the circumstances, on the conditions of China, developments in China, personalities, and so on, I shared it with the press.

When the press was allowed to go to Yenan in the spring of '44, before the army was allowed to go, people like Guenther Stein of the *Christian Science Monitor* went up there. Guenther was a very systematic, orderly person, as one might expect from his background, and he talked to me about what we wanted to know, what was valuable up there, what he should ask. Over several days we worked out a program for Guenther.

After I got to Yenan myself, the Chinese complained about what a pest Guenther Stein was, and I said, "Well, he was asking some for me." Correspondents in Yenan had been there a month or six weeks by the time we got there, and they had interviewed all the top people. Most of these correspondents made available to me their notes of all their interviews. I was able to get the information into the State Department and government channels better and faster than they could get it published.

Guenther Stein was keeping his stuff until he could write his book. But it was a very important, very productive aspect of our reporting in China. And of course, it was so productive and so useful that I got into bad habits, which got me into trouble later on.

At the end, Service referred lightly to the "trouble" he got into over the Amerasia case of 1945. The latter was a New York semi-academic monthly, which was charged with being a Communist front and raided by police in June 1945. The police found copies of reports Service had filed from Yenan. Indiscreetly perhaps, as part of his effort to keep the press informed, he had lent copies to the editor of Amerasia. A grand jury failed to indict Service, but the affair precipitated a long series of security proceedings against him which ultimately resulted in his expulsion from the State Department in the 1950s.

One of the men who replaced Service, Davies, and others after the war was over and the Nationalist government moved back to Nanking was John Melby. Melby elaborated upon Service's comments. He felt that because of the Amerasia affair, relations between the press and diplomats became noticeably more distant.

I was in the American embassy primarily as a political officer, but I had also been assigned as press attaché with the embassy and as the embassy liaison with USIS. Owing to the feeling that arose because of the *Amerasia* case, there were only two or three of us who were officially authorized to talk to the press. I was one, as press attaché, and Bradley Connors, who was the acting operational director of OWI, was another.

This isn't to say that fellow officers in the embassy and some of the consulates around didn't see press people, because they did. They just didn't talk very frankly or very freely. I thought that it was really too bad that there was this kind of inhibition on contact between the press and the people in the embassy. Using my experience, of all the press people I used to see, there was only one instance, one person, now dead, who betrayed a trust.

If I said anything was off the record or in confidence, I never had occasion to regret saying that. But it is true that after the war—because there was a change of attitude in the United States, not because of the change of attitudes in China—the relationship became more restrictive than it had been before.

However, a majority of old journalists disagreed with Melby's suggestion that the consular officials ceased cooperating with the press after 1945. Doak Barnett was perhaps the most outspoken on this point.

Many of the American consuls around the country, in places such as Sinkiang or Hankow or Kunming, were extraordinarily frank in sharing information with the press. For example, Hank Lieberman and I made a trip to Sinkiang and J. Hall Paxton there damn near opened his files to us. There are others, still living, whom I won't mention, who also virtually opened their files when I visited them. These fellows were so pleased to see another American, and I, like other correspondents, often stayed with them. So it was pretty hard to maintain a formal relationship under those circumstances. Similarly with missionaries. Especially the Catholics. You knew, incidentally, that you could always get a drink at a Catholic mission.

Phil Potter of the Baltimore Sun *seconded Barnett's comments.*

It worked both ways. We often got information that the embassy and even our military didn't have. For instance, in February 1946, I was with a group of nine correspondents, the first to get into Manchuria with the Russian army after the war. Hank Lieberman was one. Another was Charlotte Ebener. A few Americans in the Office of Strategic Services (OSS) had been allowed into Manchuria by the Russians at war's end to find and repatriate American flyers and others captured by the Japanese. But those teams had left in October at the request of the Soviet command. So the OSS had no information of what was going on, though it had maintained a post at Chinchow, 130 miles southwest of Mukden. We were in Manchuria for about two weeks, and we got a good deal of information, particularly about looting in Mukden by the Russian troops. They were putting industrial machinery taken from Japanese factories on freight cars and starting them back to Russia. A lot of the loot, of course, didn't get there. Many trains were derailed and their contents rusted away. We newsmen went on to Changchun, where we were put in custody for a while and then told to get out of Manchuria. On our return to Chinchow, I got word to General Wedemeyer in Shanghai that three of us were there. He sent his own C-54 to pick us up. When we got back to Shanghai, almost before we could even write to our home offices with what we had, he wanted me flown out to Chungking to brief General Marshall. Also sent was Arch Steele, who had arrived in Mukden after us. Quite a few hours we talked. Whereupon Marshall soon flew back to Washington.

We had a great deal of information about what the Russians were doing up there, and it was of great interest to Marshall and Wedemeyer and, I presume, the people in Washington.

Mac Fisher mentioned that such cooperation was not uncommon even prior to the Chungking years.

I'm speaking of, say, 1937 in Peking. For instance, we always checked every morning at the military attaché's office as well as the embassy, and we would confer with people there. I was a United Press correspondent at that time. I would get a hunch or a hint from somebody that something was up. I remember when we learned or guessed that the Japanese were going to attack Kalgan to the north of the Great Wall, I called Colonel Joseph Stilwell and said, "I'm going to go up there. Want to help? Can you send anybody along?" And he sent Captain Sutherland, I think it was, an artillery officer, who went along as my secretary. Because I knew enough Japanese, we got through the Japanese lines to the front where Sutherland was able to watch a Japanese field artillery battery open up against the Great Wall in the pass up there. Later Colonel Stilwell said that he was getting complaints from his fellow military attachés of other nations because he was always beating them with his reports to Washington on what was going on.

Responding to a comment that there seems to have existed a certain "enthusiasm" for sharing information among members of the American military, the diplomatic corps, and the press, Doak Barnett suggested that this was in no way unnatural or improper.

It seems to me that members of the American press corps in China at that time, as I observed them, used every possible source they could. If they could talk to Communists, they'd talk to Communists; if they could get into Communist territory, they got into Communist territory. They had extensive relationships with Kuomintang officials, and so on. They searched out any knowledgeable missionaries or any knowledgeable person of any sort. They found that American diplomats were extremely well-informed people and, therefore, they were one of the more important available sources. I would stress that members of the American press regarded any information they obtained as open information once they reported it, and therefore they shared it with anybody. So they established a two-way relationship with whoever was willing. It was a very important, mutually beneficial relationship, as I observed it.

Agreeing, Walter Sullivan added:

We were not revealing secrets, and this, I think, must be kept in mind in view of later accusations of the press playing cozy with the CIA and so forth. The information that went back and forth was open information. It was the same kind of information that you would then report to your boss and your readers.

Don Kight, Public Relations Officer (PRO) after 1944 for the US Army, agreed with the reporters and took a strong stand when it was suggested that the press should have stayed at arm's length from government officials.

Nonsense! It's a reporter's job to talk to anyone and everyone. An official was frequently the best place to start. A reporter isolated on the Salween for ten days could go to an official and get a bird's-eye view of what had been happening while he was gone. A reporter coming to Executive Headquarters would have been a damned fool if he hadn't talked to me, because I could tell him what was going on at the 39 truce team locations and give him guidance to help in his planning.

The official wanted to talk to the correspondent so *he* could do a better job. I always wanted the correspondent to talk so I could better brief the next man. (And also because I was as curious as a reporter.) That didn't mean I trotted over to the G-2 and reported the conversation to him; I didn't.

The reporter just *started* with the official. A reporter briefed by me would probably go directly to Huang Hua for the Communist side, and, after an interview with Walter Robertson, request one with General Yeh Chien-ying. Talking to officials didn't make the reporter an informal arm of the US government; it just made him a good reporter. And it didn't prevent him from writing a story the next day blasting officialdom and sending officials through the roof.

The raising of this question seems to me to indicate a gap between an academic viewpoint and the pragmatic situation on the ground and at the time. The mere physical difficulties of getting around in China, with vast distances, difficult countryside, and lack of communications, made it essential for officials and press to talk together so that both could do their jobs better.

Bill Powell also defended the need for reporters to use officials of all kinds and types as sources of information. He took issue with the implication that American official contacts might be considered contaminating because the United States was so deeply involved in the Civil War on the Kuomintang's behalf.

A reporter can't shun a potential news source because he suspects the informant's motives or finds him lacking in character. I had many a productive lunch with an amoral and immoral man involved in the opium trade in pre-Liberation Shanghai. I also had occasional meetings with the American consul general in Shanghai. The meetings with the consul general were usually less informative and certainly less lively than those with my opium man. I also regularly exchanged information with an OSS friend.

It is essential for a reporter to talk to people of all stations and persuasions. It is also acceptable to exchange information with most sources. Discussion confirms, denies, amplifies. Reporters rarely stumble on state secrets, and their information ends up either published or as background for what eventually appears in public print. Of course, the reporter can't take at face value all that the consul general or the opium dealer tells him. He has to decide whether it sounds reasonable or even possible and then check it with other sources. Unfortunately, no one is error proof, and most reporters have written at least a few stories they would just as soon forget. Caution is reinforced each time the reporter gets stung, but total immunity seems impossible.

Harrison Salisbury had the last word on the subject.

This is not exclusively a China theater matter. I was in Moscow during World War II, and I well remember that almost every morning the late Bill Lawrence, who was then the correspondent of the *New York Times*, and myself would go over to the American military attaché's office. General Deane, I think, was the man. We would go to his office, and we'd walk in and look around and look over his desk and say, "Oh, for Christ's sake, you haven't got any top secret papers here. There's nothing to read." This was our attitude, frankly. It was kind of high school, but we were all in this thing together. If we found out something interesting about the Red Army because we were out on a trip, we'd go in to Deane and say, "Well, now, geez, we saw such and such. What does that mean?" And Deane, if he saw something or got on to something, would talk to us about it.

So there were three elements. One was plain camaraderie: we were all in the same place together and we were all good fellows together. Number two, it was the war, which gave us a common goal. And number three, it was pragmatic, in that he had some things to tell us and we had some things to tell him so that it seemed to us a very normal relationship. I know that in the present-day context of the sharp dividing lines and the confrontational sort of press relationships that we have, people say, "How could that be?" Well, it was, and it was true all around the world.

Salisbury touched upon but did not sufficiently emphasize the fundamental factor behind the intimacy of the US press and government in China during the 1940s because to him and the others it seems so obvious—yet today it is easily forgotten or dismissed by later generations. There were decisive differences prevailing then that separate the war reporters of the 1940s from the foreign correspondent of the 1950s, 1960s, or today. The chief point to be remembered is that the intimacy was born of a wartime situation for which there was total public and political support in the United States. Cooperation between American military personnel and journalists not only seemed natural, it was imperative for getting their respective jobs done. Questions of propriety never came up. And after 1945, for most on both sides, a continuation of this symbiotic relationship flowed naturally out of the wartime situation.

This intimacy between the American press and government officials has been described at length for two reasons. First, it merits attention because the experience contrasts sharply with the more distant relationship prevailing in the 1950s and 1960s which was often characterized by hostility and mutual suspicion, as during the Vietnam War years. Second, and more important, an understanding of the symbiotic relationship between the press and government officials in the 1940s is critical to the evaluation of the overall policy influence of journalists in chapter 10.

5 | Newsgathering and Censorship

Reporters in Chungking overcame many obstacles that hindered both the gathering and the transmission of newsworthy stories. First, they were confronted with strong and persuasive personalities who sought to present their own version of reality to the press. Of these the most heavily interviewed were Madame Chiang Kai-shek (Soong Mei-ling) and Chou En-lai. Besides being her husband's political alter-ego, the former was American educated and the KMT's principal choreographer of relations with the West. During the war she often toured the United States, and addressed joint sessions of Congress on at least two occasions. Since the Long March of 1934–35, Chou En-lai had emerged as the Chinese Communists' chief spokesman in foreign affairs. During the war he commuted between Yenan and Chungking, remaining throughout as both a spokesman and architect of Communist policies toward the West.

Because most correspondents did not speak Chinese, they were forced to rely on interpreters and were limited in the sorts of contacts they could make.

Finally, even after the stories were written, they had to pass the extremely critical eyes of the censors, American (after 1943) as well as Chinese.

*The close relationship that developed in Chungking
between the journalists and the American officials, out-
lined in the previous chapter, demonstrated their human
side. How much, then, were these same people influenced by dominating personalities and newsmakers, such
as Chou En-lai and Madame Chiang Kai-shek? Teddy
White, in a letter sent to the conference, drew explicit attention to the "immeasurable influence on our thinking"
of people such as Chou and his public relations expert,
Kung P'eng.*

Peggy Durdin opened the discussion.

It seems to me there are enormous numbers of things
which an intelligent correspondent had to confront in the
realm of the unconscious in China. One thing certainly
was personalities. I think it is almost impossible to have
loved Madame Chiang Kai-shek, and I think that was
something that had to be dealt with. On the other hand, I
have never known a more magnetic personality than Chou
En-lai. Indeed, I was so impressed with him during the
Marshall negotiations in Nanking when Till, my husband, was temporarily on Marshall's staff, that one day he
said to me, "Peggy, now pull yourself together about Chou
En-lai." (I want to say that's one of the uses of the civil-
minded husband.)

There was nobody on the KMT side who could touch
Chou En-lai in persuasiveness or in intellectual charm,
which was a fascinating kind of charm. Nor was there
anybody on the KMT side who could touch his head of
public relations, the soft, lovely, beautiful Kung P'eng, who
was the most impressive public relations figure I ever met.

Now I'm not saying that correspondents in particular
run around getting captivated, but I think the whole fact
of unconscious reaction to events because of the qualities

of the people you get involved with is something we all have had to face.

Henry Lieberman elaborated.

Chou En-lai was one of the greatest people I've ever encountered because of his charm, his skills, his mental and dramatic ability. One of the most important things of all, I think, is that he was one of the world's greatest actors. That's how I always thought of Chou En-lai. Let me give you an example. Chou spoke poor English, so far as I could make out. I spent hour after hour with him trying to get his story. He had a trick that he'd pull, and with it I think he convinced even Kissinger that he spoke English fluently. The interpreter would go on translating for Chou, and then at some strategic point in the interview Chou En-lai would stop the interpreter, and say to him in English, "No, not that word, this word."

Arch Steele seconded the comments about Chou's personality and the believability of his accounts, as opposed to those of the Kuomintang. He also suggested that Chou had the power to manipulate correspondents' views and opinions.

As a male, I would find it difficult to say that I was captivated by Chou, although I was certainly captivated by Kung P'eng. But in discussing Chou I think we haven't really touched on the basic question of the extent to which people like Chou, and particularly Chou, manipulated the views of the correspondents in China and their coverage of Chinese events. Remember Chungking in those days and how difficult it was to get the truth about anything, how futile it was to go to the Chinese Ministry of Information to get their superficial communiqués, which could easily be disproved and were usually just nonsense. Then you would go to a little cubbyhole on the side street in Chungking that was occupied by the liaison officer of the Chinese Communists, who were then our allies, and hear from a charming person like Chou En-lai an explanation of, say, the latest conflict between the Kuomintang forces and the People's Liberation Army in some remote area of the interior, giving in great detail the facts, as he reported them, of what was going on out there. It was very tempting indeed to give considerable prominence to the detailed version and very persuasive words that we got from Chou and to more or less ignore—and quite rightly, I think, in most cases—the Nationalists' communiqués.

How candid was Chou in his interviews? Was there any perceptible difference between Chou's personal accounts and the official Communist party line? Steve Levine, a historian, phrased the question.

Did anyone, in the time spent with Chou En-lai, ever hear him utter a word that suggested that he might have differed from the party line?

Albert Ravenholt responded first.

When we got the first word in 1946 of the Russians stripping the industries of Manchuria, I asked Chou in an interview, "What do you really think about this?" And he said, "Of course, I'm opposed to this, but we can't afford to say it." This was Chou En-lai admitting that his opinion ran counter to the party line.

John Melby supported Ravenholt's account by refer-
ring to comments of Kung P'eng, Chou's public relations
officer.

She was quite frank that they didn't like what the
Russians were doing in Manchuria. In fact, she was bitter
and quite angry. "But," she said, "what do you do about it?
They're doing it. We can't stop them."

Phil Potter also remembered Chou's reaction to Rus-
sian activity in Manchuria.

I was with the group of nine correspondents who first
got into Manchuria with the Russian army and wrote
many, many stories about its stripping of Manchuria. I'd
been covering the negotiations between Marshall and
Chou En-lai for months, and I'd gotten to know Chou En-
lai very well. When I got back to Chungking, the first
thing I wanted to do was see Chou and get his attitude
on the Russian stripping of Manchuria. He would not see
me. I wrote that it was obvious that he was hostile to it;
that there was in the Chinese Communist party a minor
schism between those who had implicit faith in Russia
and those more moderate in their regard for China's northern neighbor, and that Chou was the leader of the latter
faction. The next time I went to his office, I was told he
wouldn't see me, and I never saw him again, except at
news conferences, until I left China a few months later.

Till Durdin acknowledged that he never knew Chou
to deviate from the official line and recounted the follow-
ing story:

I never found that Chou En-lai deviated from official policy. In fact, he was emphatic in showing how it changed from time to time. On one of Chou's forays abroad in the 1950s he was in Rangoon, and I happened to be there at the time. The government gave a reception for him, and I was one of the guests. As I marched through the line I met Chou, and he turned away as I offered my hand. He wouldn't shake hands. He knew me very well and I had known him very well in the Chungking days. A few months later he was in Nepal. I wasn't there at the time, but the policy had changed. He looked over the assembled correspondents to whom he was giving a press conference and said, "Where's Tillman Durdin? I don't see him." The policy had changed.

I myself became disillusioned with Chou En-lai and his group to a degree, because in the early days in Chung-king, in the propaganda war between the KMT and the Communists, the Communists were always bringing forward popular groups. They would suddenly discover the Northwest People's Political Association or the Kwei People's Political Organization or something like that. These things were made up out of whole cloth. You know, there was not a Northwest representative in Chungking or a Kwei representative in Chungking that you could get at. They were just creating all these things. And I got fed up with this kind of activity.

When asked by Dorothy Borg what he had perceived the party line to have been at the time, Durdin responded.

Well, the line vis-à-vis Russia, it seemed to me, in the Chungking days, was to say that fundamentally, "we [the Chinese Communists] have no disagreements with Soviet policies. We are our own people and we have our own way, particularly in domestic progress of the Revolution. But this does not mean that we are at cross purposes with the Soviet Union in interparty relations." This was the public posture, it seemed to me. Now as to the United States, it was to appear reasonable and moderate and to encourage relations with Americans. Chou En-lai would say, "One of my top personalities in history is Thomas Jefferson," and he would say, "One of my aspirations is to go to the United States someday, and please come to Yenan and see us," and that sort of thing. The attitude was one of courting American goodwill and good relations. Those were the two lines as I saw them.

Lieberman emphasized that personalities could be influential even when they were constrained by party doctrine.

I and many others, I'm sure, were aware of the fact that among the Communist representatives, both in Chungking and in Nanking, different personalities were imprisoned in this matrix of the party. Every once in a while the individual shone through, but part of the business of being a party member, I took for granted, was that when the decision was made about what the line was, everybody conformed or else faced party discipline. So we were always confronted with this duality.

In point of fact, the difference in personalities that emerged from people you knew gave you some indication of what the line was, so it was one very important element in dealing with a news situation. I told the story earlier about Chou En-lai and the Marshall mission and how we went to Chahar and Jehol to see whether Soviet troops were there. I want to emphasize that, after my first shock at being lied to, I came to the conclusion that this was perfectly natural behavior on the part of Chou En-lai. After all, Chou was the representative of his party in fairly important negotiations with the Nationalists, and he was trying to win every card. I didn't see or talk to Chou at the time when he was premier and foreign minister, but I'm sure that in his negotiations both with the Russians and with the United States he would do anything he thought proper in order to make his points. I think you have to make a distinction between the effect of personality on correspondents and correspondents' looking for changes in the personality of a given individual.

I think you have to look at history and developments in periodic terms, almost in a taxonomic way, classifying them as similar to this period or that period, and so on. But there are deviations. I recall a comment made by Chou En-lai about the Russians when I was trying to get his story while going on a picnic with him and his group to the Sun Yat-sen Mausoleum in Nanking. I asked him about his participation in the Marshall mission. It was then pretty clear that the Communists were likely to take over all of China and that Russia was becoming a very important factor in the situation. He made a comment along the lines that he was somewhat skittish about help from anybody. I remember this line distinctly. He said, "You're never sure of your own independence if you accept help from the outside." That is a remarkable statement from a man holding his position. In a later interview, I asked him, "Why is it that only the leaders of the Communist party can have a sense of humor and show themselves as human beings?" Well, he ducked that one, but it was true that when you engaged a high-ranking member of the party, he could afford to indulge in being himself as much as possible. The lesser members of the party could not.

Al Ravenholt reinforced Lieberman's observations on how a vibrant personality would sometimes transcend the limits of party discipline.

I think there's a dimension to history that we tend to ignore. During the war, I used to come back to Kunming after I had been covering the front in China or Burma or the Philippines, and occasionally I'd have dinner with Ho Chi Minh. This was before the 14th Air Force and the United States discovered him, and he and I would sit around and have long discussions about what was going on. He was very poor. He lived in a room that was about ten by twelve feet that was also his office, and he didn't have any maps. So I gave him some maps and things. He was a scintillating character and fun to talk with. Well, in the spring of 1946, in April, I went down to Hanoi, and saw Ho. He was still in his cloth shoes at the residence of the French superior general in Hanoi, and we had a long talk. I asked him, "Why did you make the deal with the French about letting 15,000 French troops in here, and why did you agree to stay in DeGaulle's French union?" He said, "It's my only protection from the Chinese [Nationalists]. I've got to keep control of the Chinese, and the French are going to protect me."

Then I made a mistake. At the end of about an hour and a half's discussion I said, "Oh, by the way, I'm supposed to bring you greetings from an old friend of yours." So I gave him a calling card from General Fong Fong, who had been a Communist commander in Hainan Island during the war and was then the Communist representative on Marshall's truce team at Canton. I'd been stuck there for a week and I'd been eating with them because they had a good cook. General Fong Fong said when I was heading for Hanoi, "You know, Ho Chi Minh is an old friend of mine. Let me give you a card," and he wrote it out. I said, "I know him." He said, "Never mind, you bring him this message." When I gave him this card from General Fong Fong, who's a senior Communist general in South China, Ho Chi Minh just clammed up on me. He would hardly talk. Obviously I had embarrassed him about his united front purposes and so forth. But at the end I stood up and I said, "You know, Mr. President [he was then president of the Revolutionary government over in North Vietnam] from the point of view of people like me, people like you are a hell of a lot more useful before they get into power than they are after." And he stood up, pulling on his old whiskers, and nodded, "Yes, I think what you say is true."

This is what we've got to remember about the Chinese Communists. Throughout World War II we were dealing with them during an era when they were not responsible for the management of power. It was very easy for them to be gregarious. But once you get into power, it's a different ball game.

Hugh Deane was upset by the tone of the discussion of Chou's relationship with the press.

It's obvious that Chou was a leading member of a disciplined party whose policies he was executing. To even raise the question of whether he departed from or questioned the party line seems naive and really not very useful. Very few officials in or out of that party are all that candid about the policies they are entrusted to carry out. I think that on the whole Chou combined exemplary personal standards with his own political goals successfully to a remarkable degree. And that's a view that's shared by many people in China. Of all the leaders of the party, he is the best loved and the subject of many affectionate stories.

Harrison Salisbury captured the essence of Chou En-lai's sharpness of wit in the following vignette.

We've talked of Chou En-lai here largely in terms of his effect on correspondents, which I think is natural. But if you put Chou in a slightly larger context, you know that he didn't utilize his talents only on correspondents. From my rare meetings with Chou, I have the same impression of this remarkable personality that has been expressed. I had one experience with him, accidental, which I think epitomizes a particular quality.

This was in Moscow in 1954. He had been at the Geneva Conference and had achieved, he felt, a great breakthrough for China—a breakthrough that he later regretted, because it turned out that it was not as good as he thought it was. But in any event, he was coming back through Moscow in a mood of triumph and was given a reception by the Russians at Spirodonova House. This was in the Khrushchev era, and the correspondents were invited, with all the other usual people that went to such affairs. The Russians had a rather typical caste system for receptions. There was a great central hall where the lower ranks and officials and journalists were supposed to drink their vodka and eat their caviar. Then there was a series of inner rooms which graded up in importance, and you were not supposed to leave your category room. Naturally, the only people who did leave their category room were the newspapermen. We always made a practice of sliding up to the next room and then the next and then the inner chamber, if possible. On this occasion several of us, including myself, made our usual progress. Sometimes in the past we had actually been able to get into the inner room where the guest of honor and the Politburo were entertaining. On this occasion, however, there was a guard at the door who stood with his elbow in such a way that you couldn't get past him, but you could lean past him and listen and see what was going on. So I actually leaned past him and looked, and here was the scene.

Chou En-lai was on his feet going around the room in the usual pattern of toasts. The guests were the Politburo headed by Khrushchev, at that time still including Malenkov, Bulganin, Molotov, and all the rest. There were, however, four *voyeurs* in that inner chamber. They were the ambassadors of countries that had diplomatic relations with China: the British, the French, the Indian, and I can't remember who the fourth was. The composition of this group interested me, but I was more interested in Chou. I was interested in the language he was speaking because, in spite of his poor command of English, he was offering his toast in English. Now that might not seem striking, because there were four English-speaking diplomats in the room, but the truth of the matter was that nobody in the Politburo knew a word of English. So immediately I could sense some kind of vibrations here. Chou was using English, and his toasts had to be translated from English into Russian. As I got to that door and watched, he approached Mikoyan and offered a toast to him in English. Mikoyan interrupted him rather rudely and said, "Chou, why don't you speak Russian? You speak Russian perfectly well." And Chou responded to Mikoyan, in English, saying, "Why don't you speak Chinese?" Mikoyan was considerably embarrassed, and he said, "Chinese is a very difficult language." And Chou said, "It's not that difficult. Come around tomorrow morning to the embassy. We'd be glad to give you lessons in Chinese."

At that point we were sort of shoved away from the door. But I had gotten enough, I thought, to know a number of things from this performance that obviously was not being put on for correspondents, because I don't think he realized we had pushed our unwelcome heads past the guard. It was being put on for whom? For the Russians, on the one hand, and also obviously for the foreign diplomats. And he was certainly sending a signal that you couldn't put into words exactly, although when you tell the story, I think you see what he was up to. He was demonstrating the distance and the differences between China of 1954 and the Russians. He was also delicately underlining these differences, which we later learned had made up the fabric of the relationship between these two Communist movements for years and years. All kinds of nuances went into what he was doing that day. I have always felt that this was one of his supreme accomplishments and certainly showed his acting talent at its very best. And he was enjoying every minute of it, and so was I.

Not all strong personalities presented positive images. Annalee Jacoby Fadiman remembered Madame Chiang Kai-shek.

The year 1941 was the honeymoon period. Everyone in the [Nationalist] government was brave and heroic and wonderful. At the end of my first week in Chungking I was invited to luncheon with Madame Chiang Kai-shek, who was attractive and brilliant and spoke English well (better than most Americans). She offered me a cigarette. Chinese restaurants at the time had signs saying, "A loyal Chinese will not smoke. The acreage is needed for the war effort," or some such thing. So I said, "No, thank you." By then I had changed to Chinese cigarettes which were round, lumpy, and brown, and Madame Chiang Kai-shek's Camels looked unbelievably white and beautiful. By three o'clock in the afternoon we were still talking Hollywood and girl talk, and I said, "Madame Chiang, I do smoke. I thought it would offend you. I've seen all the signs in the restaurants." She smiled beautifully and said, "Oh, that's for the people."

Everyone seemed to agree that Madame Chiang was the antithesis of Chou. She was difficult to like and lacked candor. However, Mac Fisher could remember one moment when she dropped her guard.

When I arrived in Chungking in 1941, I sought and obtained an interview with Madame Chiang. I asked her, "Don't you sometimes get tired of having to appear as the great heroic figure that everybody thinks you are?" She said, "If you ever publish this"—I never did—"I'll have your head for it. But, yes, I do get tired of it."

In spite of the visibility of Chou and Madame Chiang, several participants hastened to point out that they were by no means the only, or even the primary, source of information for reporters. Bill Powell noted other sources.

It sounds as if we had two sources of information: the Kuomintang and the Communists. Most of us found, very early on, that whatever information you got from the Kuomintang was not very good, and we began looking for other sources. And it's true that in Chungking there was a Communist headquarters with Chou En-lai, Kung P'eng, and others. But I think the main source of information was Chinese intellectuals who were dissatisfied. I never met Chou En-lai or went to one of his press conferences.

That wasn't where we got our information. We got it from a rather large group of people we met during the war. Some of them I knew in Shanghai—newspapermen, Chinese newspapermen before the war, professors, and others. You have to remember that most of the intellectuals were disenchanted with the Kuomintang. These were the people you relied on. You knew them over a period of years, and after a while you began to know which were almost invariably correct and which were of very little use. A large number of ordinary, nongovernmental figures gave us most of our information.[1]

Till Durdin supported Powell's statement and cautioned the listeners not to overemphasize the journalistic impact of the more dominant personalities.

The point has been made that Madame Chiang, the Generalissimo, and many of the higher officials had impacts that were negative rather than affirmative. But there were good, honorable, honest sources on the Kuomintang side. You could get an objective, honest analysis, for example, from Hu Shih, Chiang Mon-lin, Chiang T'ing-fu, and Fu Ssu-nien. These people were able to put the Kuomintang case in historical and political perspective that helped me at least to understand, if not approve, the policies of the Kuomintang. They played the same role as Chou En-lai and his spokesmen on the other side.

Doak Barnett also underlined Powell's observation.

I got there in 1947, and I hasten to say that I spent most of my time out in the provinces, not in Shanghai and Nanking. But my impression was that in Shanghai, Nanking, and Peking too, people like those in the Democratic

League were among the main sources that shaped the environment in which the foreign correspondents were operating. People interviewed Kuomintang officials, and they tried to have contacts with the Communists, but the people whom the correspondents had most contact with were university people, intellectuals, and the like, most of whom were connected with the Democratic League. If you look at that group and its interaction with the press, you will find a very major influence on foreign reporting in China at that time.[2]

The discussion on information sources led naturally to the issue of the importance of having a command of the Chinese language. Wilma Fairbank put the question to the assembled journalists.

Among all of you, perhaps one or two had been born in China and may have spoken Chinese fluently, but most of you had to depend on translators, English-speaking individuals who, in effect, played the part that compradores did for the early tea trade businessmen in China. Therefore, you were once removed, in a sense, from the people you were interviewing. Even when you had firsthand experiences, you presumably had to discuss them and analyze them with the person you were dealing with. And if they were English-speaking individuals, they already had some kind of a change in mind set from their original Chinese mind set. I would like very much to know how this may have affected your work.

Henry Lieberman acknowledged the handicap but pointed out that it was only one of many deficiencies with which one learned to reckon.

I suffered from not having a China background and from inability to handle the language as well as I would have liked. Nevertheless, this kind of thing can be carried too far, because the type of reporting and analysis required in China is separate from language skill, at least to my way of thinking. Obviously, knowing the language and the history is vital, but that doesn't by itself qualify you to take a look at a country in all of its aspects and deal with it properly as a reporter. It has become increasingly important to be able to come to grips with all the fundamental aspects of what makes a nation. There is, of course, the culture of the country. But the culture is more than the art objects; it is the quality and feel and the values of the people. In addition to that, now that so much of the Far East is industrializing, it is vital to be able to analyze hardball politics, national interests, conflicting interests, conflicting values, the momentum of international events, and so on. A modern correspondent really has to be a Renaissance man. And we all know there is no longer any such thing as a Renaissance man.

Annalee Jacoby Fadiman acknowledged that not being able to speak Chinese limited her ability to travel to certain parts of the country.

I can remember quite well how much it affected our work, although most of us spoke at least some Chinese. But there were so many of the Chinese officials who had been educated at American colleges that most of the cabinet, many of the generals, welcomed us because they'd had the American experience. Almost everywhere we went, someone did speak English. Of course, we were limited. We never knew about the places where we couldn't have met an English speaker. We never missed them because we didn't know about them. But there were democratic groups or education groups where one person spoke English and would help us. And we were terribly dependent upon our interpreters. Ours—Teddy White's, John Hersey's, and mine—was the bravest, most intelligent, most delicate, fragile young woman, who I think was bound to make us love China even more than we did. Because we didn't miss what we didn't know, we felt as though almost all of China was open to us. Our terrible Chinese was enough for elementary questions in a lot of places. We should have felt limited, probably, but we didn't. Not very much.

Doak Barnett then drew a sharp line of distinction between fluency in Chinese and being a good journalist and reporter.

There's no doubt that lack of fluency in the language had some adverse effects. We have discussed some of them, including the dependence of correspondents on interpreters and the English-speaking Chinese intellectual groups. They were very important intermediaries between non-Chinese-speaking Americans and the rest of Chinese society. Having said that, I also feel compelled to say something that a lot of my academic peers are going to react against automatically. That is, there is no direct correlation, in my observation, between knowledge of the language and being a first-rate correspondent.

Many of the best reporters in China were people who had special qualities that made them good reporters even though they didn't have the language. They had to cope with that liability and work through all kinds of intermediaries, and they did. But the qualities that made them good correspondents were a searching mind, an inquiring mind, curiosity, a dedication to digging out facts, and a sense of balance; some of the people who knew the language didn't have those qualities. So it's not easy to deal with this question. Not knowing the language was a liability for many people, but people were able, to a remarkable degree, to overcome it. If they had spent five years learning the language, I'm not sure that they would necessarily have been the best reporters.

The question was asked whether there were cases of being misled by the interpreter or translator. The consensus was that such dissimulation was easy to identify and would have discredited the perpetrator as a reliable source. Till Durdin explained:

Other channels enabled us to check up on our translators. We received translations of broadcasts from the Communist areas, translations from the Kuomintang areas and the Kuomintang press through the embassy and other channels. They gave us enough background so that I don't think our Chinese assistants were able to mislead us even if they wanted to.

Bill Powell concurred, referring to the translation projects engaged in by his father and himself:

We solved, or tried to solve, this problem with translation services, and I think ours was much better than the consulate's. We'd have every major paper in town, any article of importance, in the office by ten o'clock that morning, and once a week we had a translation of fifty or sixty pages of all the Chinese magazines. In that sense it was a way of overcoming the language problem. The USIS had a translation service, as did the Jesuit scholars and the American Chamber of Commerce. All were available to the correspondents. Learning Chinese is not like learning French. It is a formidable language and my experience has been that, with few exceptions, even our best China scholars feel more confident using Chinese interpreters when conducting important interviews.

Julian Schuman, a competent linguist and collector of colloquialisms, is a treasure trove of stories about the language. His account, perhaps apocryphal, of an early Henry Kissinger–Alexander Haig visit to Peking has General Haig out for a morning walk with two top State Department language experts. They see a man standing at the edge of the sidewalk looking them over, and Haig says: "Go ask him what happened to Lin Piao." They tell Haig that the man's reply makes no sense, just two strange words. Back at the guest house dictionaries are consulted to no avail. What the man said, Julian explains, was what everybody in Peking was saying at the time. They were the key words from a Chinese proverb used to describe the departure from this world of an unloved character. The pedestrian had simply said "belch fart," a sort of Chinese acronym for "He belched and he farted, and he went to meet the King of Hades."

The idea that American reporters should have gone into the countryside to talk with the peasants sounds reasonable, but in practice it wasn't productive. I tried this a number of times with Chinese and Western friends. All we ever found out was that conditions were bad, which we already knew. Attempts to get answers to detailed questions failed. I think this was because the peasants were not willing to unburden themselves to a stranger, especially a foreigner. Besides, the range of their knowledge was limited.

The peasants made the revolution, but it was under the direction of intellectuals who were sensitive to the people's needs. A better way to find out what life was like in the countryside was to read Fei Hsiao-t'ung's books on peasant life and then spend long hours talking with him and other knowledgeable Chinese.

On the other hand, "hanging around the cities" did have its rewards. Shortly after the end of World War II, President Truman sent former president Herbert Hoover on an around-the-world fact-finding mission on food. The Shanghai Famine Relief Commission hosted the Hoover party with a welcome dinner at a local hotel. As usual with such affairs, word got out, and I had to push through a crowd of perhaps three hundred destitute refugees blocking the door and half of Nanking Road, all crying for food and money.

It was an excellent many-course dinner on the top floor with a good view of the race course. The food high point was a roast suckling pig at each of twenty or so large tables. I can still remember how perfectly it was done, the crisp skin scored in squares just the right size to remove with chopsticks for dipping in the plum sauce. The high point of the speeches was the one by the head of the local relief committee who expressed his deep appreciation to the American president who had sent the world's foremost relief expert to help China. His country, he said, was desperately short of food, and many people did not have enough to eat. He hoped US aid would arrive soon. By the time the dinner was over, the crowd in the street had swelled and it was necessary to really push and shove to get clear. It was unpleasant on a full stomach.

Having spent years acquiring a mastery of the language and more years studying China's history, the historian can easily take a jaundiced view of the reporter's usually less impressive academic credentials, hasty work, and vast (by academic standards) output of words, admittedly sometimes not as judiciously weighed as they might be. There are few who can work both sides of the street. Anna Louise Strong was an academic and also a good reporter. John Fairbank is also unusual. Besides scholarly work, he produces newspaper articles that are models of clarity.

Some things cannot be taught in school, and the reporter discovers the real world very quickly. He learns to spot stuffed shirts, con men, people on the make, the well-intentioned, the put-upon, and all the rest who make up the human population. It is understandable that public figures complain about the press and often claim they were misquoted or quoted out of context. The reporter's insistent and probing questions can be disconcerting, but they are necessary to help expose bureaucratic dissimulations and to clarify confused or complicated issues.

Israel Epstein offered an observation on the misuse of Chinese language ability.

In the early stages of the war, and even before the war between China and Japan, undoubtedly the best-informed people, the best-equipped in terms of language, were the Japanese. They knew an immense amount. They could circulate in China, they could be mistaken for Chinese if they wanted to and if they spoke the language well enough. And then they got it hopelessly wrong. Most American correspondents, ill equipped as they were, could see that the Japanese couldn't win a war in China. The Japanese couldn't see that, because they had a vested interest in this war. You may be badly informed but you may see the main things; on the other hand, you may not want to look at certain things, so you're not going to see them.

Frederick "Fritz" Marquardt supported the position that language knowledge is not an essential prerequisite for good journalism with a quip about Owen Lattimore.

I traveled once for a month with Owen Lattimore when we were both working for the OWI. We were on our way to Australia, and Owen could order a much better meal at a Chinese restaurant than I could. But I doubt very much that he was as good a reporter as I was in those days.

Mary Sullivan also played down the importance of foreign language fluency.

When you got out in the countryside you really did have to have an interpreter unless you knew the language. But more of the KMT officials spoke English than did the Communists. Outside of a couple of Communist superstars, there was much broader access to Kuomintang officials, most of whom spoke English.

Second, another English-speaking source was the returned Chinese students. I remember going to a lunch of Columbia University alumni and meeting some of them.

Third, the correspondents mingled easily with Chinese friends. So I don't think that they were dependent even on their own staff. There was much social interchange with Chinese intellectuals, as has been mentioned, with Chinese newspaper people who spoke English, and to a lesser degree with some of the students who were studying English, and to whom you could talk. Language ability is perhaps more needed now than it was back then when things were a great deal more fluid and open.

Even Jack Belden, who acquired a sound command of the Chinese language de-emphasized its importance as a journalistic tool.

I would have to say that the language isn't very important to a reporter's job. It is important if you want to understand the Chinese people and their culture, but this is not the purpose of most reporters' work. Knowing the language can be an advantage in times of crisis when people are more likely to talk freely than when the government is in control. But from 1946 to 1948, as far as I know, I was the only journalist in the Chinese countryside and even I didn't get the information I wanted—too much bureaucracy.

John Service then reminded everyone that knowledge of the language was, nevertheless, a great aid.

Yes, being a good reporter may be more important than knowing the language. Nonetheless, having command of the language gives you more mobility. If you don't have the language, you're pretty much tied to Peking or Nanking or Chungking. If you're able to get along, then you can get out into the countryside if you're lucky. But you also can hear people talking on the street, you overhear a conversation on a bus, you can read signs and posters.

John Fairbank brought the discussion to a close.

Somebody should point out that reporting from China occurred not only in the press but in diplomatic channels, and there's been a very modest statement from a diplomatic reporter of that time [John Service] who remarks that if you can understand what the people are saying, perhaps you can understand what's in their minds. And, thank God, such a person was there. His reports are historic, and I think there's no question that those of us working in the press and other parts of the government could have done better if we had had his linguistic capacity. And we didn't, so it's a black mark. We couldn't do what he could do.

Another prominent theme that affected the reporting of news in China was censorship. A persistent observation was that Chiang Kai-shek's news censorship contributed greatly to the erosion of confidence in his regime as the war dragged on.

Hugh Deane began by recounting the censorship imposed on the reporting of the New Fourth Army Incident in 1941.

I was in Chungking during the critical New Fourth Army Incident. As you know, Kuomintang troops attacked a rear section of the New Fourth Army, which had been ordered to move north of the Yangtze River, killing and arresting many. For the moment it seemed as if Kuomintang-Communist relations were going to break up right then. During the weeks before the actual attack, Jack Belden and I, and sometimes one or two others, went several times a week to the Communists' city office to question Chou En-lai or one of his aides, Ch'en Chia-k'ang or Kung P'eng. Censorship made getting the story out difficult. Belden typed his principal story twice, making a total of perhaps eight copies, giving them to different people flying out to Hong Kong. But all of us in Chungking were beaten on the New Fourth Army story by Edgar Snow and others in Hong Kong and elsewhere.

On the day that word reached the Communists of the

attack on the New Fourth, their Chungking paper, the *Hsin-hua jih-pao*, defied censorship and ran a poem and an emotional comment by Chou. I remember getting the issue, printed on green paper. But it and some other papers and photos were taken from my room during an air raid. (The Kuomintang police habitually took advantage of the raids, while we sat in shelters in tunnels, to search correspondents' rooms.)

During those early months of 1941, Belden and I and one or two others were kept busy trying to get the specifics on the suppression of opponents of the Kuomintang, real and suspected. Daily I tried to track down leftists, liberals, and other dissidents and interview them. People were arrested, book shops were raided. Some fled to Kwangsi or Hong Kong. Ma Yin-ch'u, a distinguished economist and chief critic of the Kuomintang's economic policies, was arrested and taken to Kweiyang; years later he was to be persecuted again, this time by the Communist regime. One by one my sources and Belden's dried up. My articles often did not get out but wound up in the drawer of Hollington Tong's desk.

Anyway, I went home in the spring of 1941 with my notebooks full of heavy stuff on the oppression and Kuomintang-Communist relations. Chou En-lai and his aides gave me a farewell dinner at which Chou handed me a map showing the areas where Kuomintang and Communist troops had clashed and confronted each other. I still have it.

The *Monitor* commissioned a series of ten articles under the general title "Inside the War." I wrote one or two and came forth with a lot of hot rhetoric. The *Monitor's* distinguished foreign editor, Charles E. Gratke, called me in, sat me down, and said, "Hugh, if you write for *The Nation*, you can call a spade a spade. But at the *Monitor* it's a little trowel." He wanted me to say everything, but with restraint. Taking advantage of his specific criticisms I wrote ten pieces, and it was all there. The theme of the series incidentally was that the Kuomintang had blown its opportunity to take advantage of the people's patriotism and wish for unity, and that it had no mass support and was on its way out. I wound up by saying that the Communists had won the battle for the minds of the peasants, and I suggested that this was going to be the decisive factor.

Hollington Tong, a graduate of the Missouri School of Journalism, was the man responsible for enforcing China's censorship laws. His heavy-handed methods were illustrated by Israel Epstein's anecdote.

When a group consisting of Harold Isaacs of *Newsweek*, Chris Hopper of the *Shanghai Evening Post and Mercury* and ABC, and Clyde Farnsworth of AP filed applications to go to Yenan after October 1945, they were denied. Holly, as we called him, said, "I favored this ban myself, in part in fairness to the correspondents. It seemed to me far better to refuse the permission outright than to permit them to take the trip and then apply wholesale censorship to their dispatches."
How considerate of him.

Other illustrations of Tong's methods related by Epstein dated back to 1942.

Teddy White had visited Wong Wen-hao (geologist and minister of interior) to get the story of the Yumen oilfields for *Time*. Wong told him that when the fields were about to be opened in 1938, it was found that the only drilling machinery in that part of the country had fallen into the hands of the Red Army during its advance in North Shensi. So Wong Wen-hao approached Chou En-lai about the equipment. Chou said, "Of course we will hand it over to you. We have been keeping it till China needed it." And he did hand it over. When White turned in the message containing this story, Tong grew livid. He called White in and declared: "This cannot be sent. Can't you see that the Communists will use it in their propaganda abroad?" "But the minister gave it to me," said White. "The minister may have, but he had no right to give a newspaperman secret state information. Maybe he wants to take responsibility before the Generalissimo if it goes out. Then it's okay." Right there, Tong picked up the receiver and called Wong. Wong admitted he had given the information but suddenly asked, "Let me hear White's story. Has he any figures on oil production?" "Yes," said Tong, "of course he had some." "Then," said Minister Wong, saving both his face and the situation, "you'd better kill the message. We can't have figures go out."

Later, in 1942, Karl Eskelund of the United Press got a statement from Chou En-lai after the latter's talk with Wendell Willkie, in which Chou expressed the opinion that the mutual understanding that had marked the Willkie talks was a good augury for KMT-Communist rapprochement. Chou himself read over the translation, and Joe Barnes (New York Herald Tribune editor and guide to Willkie) showed it to Willkie, endorsing it, "This is okay with Mr. Willkie." But Tong took one look at this endorsed copy and blew up. He crossed out Chou's statement in its entirety "for reasons given on separate sheet." On the separate sheet he scrawled that way back in 1937 the Communist party had agreed absolutely to obey the Generalissimo in all things, and that therefore there could be no talk of "relations" or "rapprochement," only of obedience. The whole statement was therefore nothing but Communist propaganda. Eskelund wanted to keep both documents—the message with Barnes's own okay and the censor's elision, and the "separate sheet" with the reasons—to show to Barnes and Willkie. But he was apparently overheard talking about this, because the whole exhibit suddenly disappeared without trace from his desk.

For some reason the New Life Movement, and "prestige" of the kind that used to make them forbid photographs of shabbily dressed coolies, suddenly came into play. At Tungkwan, the Generalissimo's son Chiang Wei-kuo drank a toast with visitors in captured Japanese wine. This was struck out of all cables. A Chinese officer doesn't drink. But when the shouts became too loud, the "official version" appeared in *Central News*. It stated, "By the order of his superior officer, Captain Chiang Wei-kuo drank a toast." No doubt he didn't like it and had to force himself! Anyhow, it was allowed to be sent out only in these words. The acme of *amour propre* was reached when Tong crossed the word "brass" out of the news that Willkie was welcomed with brass bands in Sian. The word "brass" seemed to him to be somehow derogatory to China!

Epstein reminded his listeners that if the Kuomintang regulations had been followed to the letter, practically nothing could have been reported.

No mention was permitted in news dispatches from foreign correspondents about Kuomintang-Communist differences, the existence of cliques or quarrels within the Kuomintang, the movements and personal life of the Generalissimo, his book *China's Destiny* and direct quotations therefrom, and subjects such as the corruption of public officials. In economic matters, the subject of inflation was forbidden, both specifically and generally, and the description of the economic situation as being serious or critical was forbidden. Correspondents could not mention that any Chungking street was dirty. Obviously, censorship couldn't be applied totally because nothing would have come back from Chungking.

Epstein also recalled an incident that illustrated how American censors affected reporting by treating Communist territory as synonymous with territory held by the Japanese.

There was a pilot from Boston named Lieutenant Joe Baglio who was shot down somewhere near Peking by the Japanese. He landed in Communist guerrilla territory, and was brought back to Yenan and on to Kunming. I wrote a dispatch about this, but it was killed on the general grounds that escape routes and escapes should not be written about.

John Service, agreeing with Epstein, protested this decision in vain to his superiors at the time in the following words:

Our ban on stories of American pilots coming down in Communist-controlled areas is based on very different conditions existing in other parts of the world. It serves no useful purpose as far as the safety or continued rescue of pilots in North China is concerned, and it works against our broad interests by assisting the Kuomintang to conceal from the public, knowledge of Communist strength and usefulness.

It would appear that the Baglio story was killed in accordance with regulations referring to "enemy-occupied territory" and "occupied China."

I suggest that the matter can be clarified by recognition of the obvious fact that most of the territory through which Baglio traveled was not enemy-occupied. He came down in guerrilla territory where the Japanese were operating but not in complete occupation. From that he passed into a large Communist base where there were no Japanese forces whatsoever. Here he traveled openly, by day, with only a small escort, which was more to guide than protect him. In this section the towns held public celebrations to welcome him. On his way out, he went from *Chinese-controlled* to *Chinese-controlled* bases by passing through narrow strips where the Japanese were confined to block-houses.

The assumed intention of censorship is to conceal information from the enemy. But our censorship of the fact that American fliers are able to land in and come out of Communist areas in north, central, and south China conceals nothing that the enemy does not already know, and only keeps our own public uninformed of facts of significant interest. Baglio's story could and should have been released because it was of great news and human interest and would have given the American public a vivid picture of actual conditions on the war front in North China. This encouraging picture of active resistance and Chinese-American cooperation is all the more desirable because of the gloomy news the American public is now receiving from the rest of China. All that needed elimination was certain place-names (where he came down and where he crossed railways) and Baglio's own name if thought advisable because of possible continued duty in the theater.

The elimination of these details would not have detracted from the value and news interest of the story.

Epstein told how the Kuomintang imposed its censorship policies on the radio airwaves.

Because of Chungking's isolated situation and because of the cost of press dispatches and the limited cable facilities, the correspondents had the use of the Chungking radio. Each of us could use it once a week for a dispatch of about 1,500 words. Like a radio mailing, this was sent out over XGOY, the Chungking international radio station. This was a very useful facility, and broadcasts were picked up by a dentist in Ventura, California, Dr. Charles Stewart, who was a "ham," or amateur radio operator, and sympathetic to China. He would pick these things up and then mail them out to wherever they were supposed to go. But this was on a reward and punishment basis. If you wrote things that the Kuomintang wasn't very happy about, they would withdraw this facility for a week or two.

Al Ravenholt recalled an incident in which the American government censored dispatches from him and from Brooks Atkinson of the New York Times.

We spent some months on the Salween River front in southwestern China. We had a couple of pack animals and Chinese soldiers, and we walked up and down the mountains visiting various parts of the front. When the troops we were with crossed a certain pass, we found that the Japanese had cannibalized their own casualties. They had been eating them for three or four weeks before the Chinese finally captured the establishment. The American government pulled my dispatch on the Japanese use of cannibalism, although I never understood why.

We had other kinds of censorship in which the Americans as well as the Chinese Nationalists were involved. One example concerns the whole question of Russia's entry into the Far East. In either late May or early June of 1945, Harrison Salisbury sent a curious message to me in Chungking: "Any likelihood that Shapiro will be needing maps in your bailiwick? Please advise." Well, Shapiro was the United Press bureau chief in Moscow, and this was Harrison's way of circumventing the censorship. I sent back a cable to New York saying, "Yes, sometime before my birthday. Check with so and so." My birthday is the ninth of September. In other words, I concluded that Russia was coming into the war in the Far East, but I wasn't allowed to write about it.

Questions about the vagaries of US and Chinese censorship at work were raised by historian Michael Schaller in reference to the recall in October 1944 of General Joseph Stilwell.

Although many journalists later described in detail the operations of wartime censorship and how they struggled against it to file the Stilwell story, only veiled references to the problems of censorship appeared in contemporary newspaper and magazine stories at the time. Clearly, however, something had happened to US military and Chinese censorship during the Stilwell crisis which allowed controversial stories to appear. (The *Christian Science Monitor* did publish a brief note that its China correspondent, Guenther Stein, could not get his story out of China. *Newsweek* and the *New York Times* both revealed that their reporters "struggled" to get their stories out.) On this issue and others, it would be extremely helpful to know how KMT and US military censorship operated between 1941 and 1945. How and when were rules tightened or relaxed? Did the US military, in sympathy with Stilwell, loosen controls? Were they tightened under General Wedemeyer?

The journalists did not respond specifically to Schaller's questions but they continued to unwind generally on the subject of press censorship by the American side. Bill Powell's censorship difficulties, for example, stemmed primarily from the American government and were caused by his editorial policies while publishing the China Weekly Review.

The *Review* had quite a bit of influence despite its small circulation. It was, of course, closed after Pearl Harbor. I reopened it in 1945. Something out of every issue was quoted in Chinese papers. I have a great, fat clipping book of the stories that were reprinted in the Chinese press out of the *Review.* It was even quoted abroad. So I think it had more influence than its circulation would indicate.

Every now and then the Kuomintang would give us a little trouble, but we always managed to get around it. That is, until shortly before the fall of Shanghai when the KMT censored all papers. We ended up with another kind of problem. We continued publishing after 1949, and I thought that things would settle down, that there would be recognition by the United States, that trade would resume, that Shanghai would continue as an important port, and that there would be a foreign community there with businessmen and others. Well, it was a very poor reading of the political tea leaves, so we kept having more and more difficulty keeping the *Review* going. If there's not censorship, you have the problem with the advertisers. We had some economic services and translation services, so we survived through the Korean War.

Shortly after we came home in 1953, Sylvia and Julian Schuman and I had our run-ins with investigative committees and then eventually the three of us were indicted for sedition in San Francisco. The thirteen charges against me added up to $130,000 and 260 years. Some of them were quite interesting. One of them said that I had written that Chiang Kai-shek was corrupt and a pawn of the United States government. After each charge it said that I knew these things to be untrue, but printed them anyway in an effort to interfere with the success of American arms. Well, we fought this for a number of years, and we eventually won. Then the government charged the three of us with treason and tried to keep us in jail, that being a capital crime. But that dragged on, and so, really from about 1954 to 1961, when the Kennedy administration finally gave up, we paid our sort of censorship price.

Another twist on the types of stories censored by the American government was given by Mary Sullivan, who was employed by the USIS in 1946.

We were doing everything we could to assure the supremacy of the Nationalist government. After the end of World War II, we continued to give aid to the Nationalist government. The USIS was receiving a news file that was written in Washington and sent to us in China. We translated it into Chinese and put it out on the network that John Fairbank and Mac Fisher talked about, where it went to the fourteen or fifteen USIS branch offices in China.

During the Marshall mediation mission, General Marshall went to Nanking to get some agreement between the Communists and the Nationalists. He did not want the extent of United States aid to the Nationalist government known. We in the USIS were not permitted to circulate one word of anything, which meant that we were, in essence, censoring reports of Secretary of State Byrnes to Congress that dealt with any congressional action on appropriations for China.

Don Kight was public relations officer (PRO) for the United States Army after VJ Day, following the move from Chungking to Shanghai and the KMT reoccupation of eastern China. In 1946 he served the Marshall mission in Peking, remaining there until after the Communist takeover in 1949. Kight's perspective on press censorship differed from the correspondent's view. He began by saying that no reporters received special treatment.

It should be remembered that most military public relations officers were really civilians, with the civilian concept of openness and freedom of the press. Many were professional journalists, in "for the duration." Our training and instincts were to treat all press equally.

I felt it was my duty to answer a question from Anna Louise Strong as quickly and fully as one from the *New York Times*. I sent a Tass man to Mukden in one of the two seats allocated to me on the courier flight from Marshall's executive headquarters in Peking.

The only exceptions I can think of to my rule were these:

When Stilwell was recalled, I received from Chungking (I was in Kunming) the only censorship instructions I ever got during the war, to the general effect of "Do not allow correspondents to mention politics in connection with recall of General Stilwell." I showed this to the American correspondents around that day (Al Ravenholt was one) despite its classification. I would not have shown it to non-American correspondents. (Those to whom I showed it broke up in laughter and promised to comply— having already made arrangements to smuggle their copy across the Hump to India for filing.)

A second instance I can recall was in Shanghai right after the Japanese surrender. Reporters from all over the world popped up through holes in the sidewalk. Among them, I discovered, were a couple who had collaborated with the Japanese, Tokyo Rose fashion. Them I gave nothing.

And a third incident occurred at Marshall's executive headquarters in Peking. The Communist public relations officer—whose name happened to be Huang Hua— wouldn't cooperate. I had a release, already approved by the Nationalist public relations officer, which was nothing more than the announcement of a new commander for one of the truce teams out in the countryside. Despite two or three hours of argument in his hotel room, Huang Hua would not approve. Thenceforth, when I had a piece of news, I saved argument by passing it out—but not to Communist newsmen. (Huang Hua had been passing out information and propaganda long before I started.)

During the executive headquarters period, the many generals for whom I worked and Chargé d'Affaires Walter Robertson were not, for the most part, particularly fond of the press. However, after 1940 few officers reached flag rank without some appreciation of the role of the press in American society, and none of them gave me much trouble. During the Salween campaign, for example, General Dorn had me sit in on planning sessions with the

Chinese chief of staff—just the three of us—which generally started at midnight and lasted three or four hours. The information garnered here was invaluable in briefing correspondents who stayed in my press tent while covering the fighting. I can recall no case where "my" generals (or Mr. Robertson) turned down a request for an interview.

I didn't have much to do with censorship, except for some run-ins with G-2 (Intelligence) where G-2 was usually overruled by the current general. However, in a press hostel I ran in Kunming there were two censors across the courtyard, subsidiary to Chungking. These officers were also civilians in for the duration and had a civilian attitude toward censorship. They had a list of taboos from [Theater headquarters in] Chungking—troop movements, for instance—but in my observation they were very liberal in their interpretations. Once in a great while I would be dragged across the courtyard and into an argument, usually arguing for the reporter. The score was probably pretty even in the long run.

There really wasn't much for the Americans to censor (the Chinese censorship was a different matter). If a reporter wanted to cover the Salween, he stayed at my press tent in Paoshan, where I was sufficiently informed through my midnight conferences and trips to the field to brief him, and where General Dorn would always grant interviews (while G-2 stood shaking his head).

I would then take the correspondent anywhere he wanted to go either by jeep or walking. (The area of interest was spread out and among ranges of six- to eight-thousand foot mountains traversed only by narrow trails, except for the Burma Road itself.) A reporter trying to do an intelligent story on the campaign would be isolated for a week or ten days, knowing practically nothing of what was happening elsewhere in China or in the world.

In essence, there wasn't any censorship during this period. After the war, of course, formal censorship disappeared (American censorship, at least).

At executive headquarters in Peking there was scant censorship at the source. The chargé d'affaires, Walter Robertson, was very open with the press and would always grant interviews. This doesn't mean he didn't keep to himself some information about high-level meetings with his Nationalist and Communist counterparts, but he was remarkably open.

Reporters who wanted to visit one of the 39 truce teams from Jehol to Canton were able to ride the weekly courier plane, although they had to line up, for I only had two seats a month reserved for me. To the best of my knowledge, they were received openly by the American-led teams. Interest, of course, centered on General Marshall's activities in Nanking, and visitors to executive headquarters were in and out, with only a few stationed there.

To sum up, as far as I am aware American censorship during the entire decade was no problem, although I'm sure every reporter on the list has at least one horror story.

For the most part, the news did get out of China, although it was often delayed. The stories filed by the correspondents were accurate and incisive, considering the handicaps faced by the journalists. But, having survived the censors, the news story had one more major challenge to face before reaching the American reader and that was the gatekeeper or editor waiting in the home office.

The Gatekeepers:
Deciding What Finally
Reaches the Reader

Getting the news out of the country was only one aspect
of informing the American public about what was hap-
pening in China. James D. White, a long-time reporter
and editor for the Associated Press, put it this way:

I'd like to respond to John King Fairbank, who reminded the correspondents that they had been involved in
a failure in China when the Communist-led revolution
took over the country after the truce efforts failed, and to
Henry Lieberman who said that in his opinion the 1940s
press corps in China had done a good job. I'd go further:
from my 1940s experience, I'd say they did a surprisingly
good job, taking into account all the difficulties, and that
the policy failure occurred partly because not enough attention was paid to what was being reported.

I offer this opinion because, although I was in China
only during the beginning and toward the end of the decade, I spent the rest of it either in Washington, D.C.,
working with familiar sources from China, or later in San
Francisco dealing with floods of copy from China, little of
which got into print. During this decade the central problem about news from China seems to me to have been
not the reporting itself, but what happened to it after it

reached this country. And what happened to it often had little to do with the importance or accuracy of the information. Instead, its fate many times was decided from among two sets of factors which still influence the information media in this country and which most people rarely think about. One set reflects the pressures inherent in the need of the information media to succeed economically. The other set stems from the polarized assumptions underlying the formation of American public opinion which already in the 1940s were contributing to the climate for the Cold War.

The uncertain fate awaiting news from China was further described by F. McCracken (Mac) Fisher, who was United Press correspondent in Peking, Shanghai, and Chungking until he established the USIS office in Chungking, soon after Pearl Harbor.

In China, once the correspondent had acquired, sifted, and evaluated the news, succeeded in getting his dispatch past the censors, and arranged its transmission to the United States, he could do no more. But other "gates" had to be passed before his story reached the American reader. Over these he had no control. At each gate the dispatch could be passed without change, could be abbreviated, could be rewritten to include material from other sources, could be materially altered by the gatekeeper, or could be killed entirely.

If the correspondent worked for a news agency, the first gate would be the agency's cable desk in New York or San Francisco, where the cable editor would evaluate the story according to how well he thought it would "sell" to the editors of client papers. The temptation to dramatize a story, to enliven or shorten it by rewriting, was always present. The second gate was the newspaper editor, always keen to increase circulation by providing stories and headlines that would boost street sales, without using too much limited copy space.

If the correspondent worked for one of the major metropolitan dailies or a magazine, the agency cable desk gatekeeper was eliminated, and decisions would be made by the foreign news editor. Although there were notable exceptions, publications with their own correspondents in China were less apt to ignore, abbreviate, or alter the dispatches which already had cost them so much. The exceptions were owners or editors with "policies" of their own which did not always square with the accounts coming out of China, even from their own correspondents. Such individuals—like Luce and Chambers of *Time*—were fortunately few in number, but disastrously influential in the shaping of public opinion.

Don Kight elaborated on the roles played by gatekeepers.

When Pearl Harbor happened, the knowledge of China held by most Americans consisted of Marco Polo, O-lan and the locusts (from *The Good Earth*), Fu Manchu, Charlie Chan (who was an American), and pennies contributed in Sunday school toward missionary efforts. At the end of the war, their knowledge consisted of Marco Polo, O-lan and the locusts, Fu Manchu, Charlie Chan (still an American), and billions contributed to that pretty Mrs. Chiang who made speeches to Congress.

The Americans in uniform who went to China were few compared to those who went to Europe and the Pacific. They were civilians whose basic objective was to get the war over with, get home as fast as possible, and get out of uniform. They weren't much interested in China. They formed two opinions. The first was that the Gimo's army was nothing to brag about. To prove this, all they had to do was walk out of Hostel One in Kunming and see "recruits" lashed together by rope, their ranks depleted by fifty percent casualties in the thousand-mile march from their place of "recruitment." The second opinion was based on rumor—the Communists headquartered in Yenan were fighting the Japanese.

In view of their objective of getting the war over with as quickly as possible, they were anti-Chiang and pro-Communist. This had nothing whatsoever to do with ideology. They were apolitical, completely. So were most of the regular military. (There were exceptions; there were always exceptions.) Not only were most of the military apolitical, but the Russian Communists were allies, so why couldn't the Chinese Communists be?

However, this group of Americans was so minuscule in terms of the entire American force overseas that their opinions didn't influence the amount of coverage devoted to China by the editors of the Mineral Wells (Texas) *Index*, the Keyser (W.Va.) *Daily News*, or the weekly known as *The Hampshire Surprise*, so named because the reader never knew what he'd see in it this week.

Plenty of copy was coming out of China, but in most papers it amounted to a short paragraph in a long war story, scarcely enough to influence public opinion. Hometown stories, curiously, gained enormous space. Usually they were run in toto. They had a deep impact, but a very narrow one, limited to family and friends. The larger papers printed numerous stories, but they were a drop in the bucket compared with coverage of Europe and the Pacific. I know of only one editorial on the Salween campaign, in the *New York Times* for 24 March 1945.

The point of all this is that although an ample supply of copy was coming out of China, the editors and other gatekeepers didn't run very much of it. Few Americans were involved, and few Americans had roots—and therefore an interest—in China. Gatekeepers felt no pressure to run copy.

As for books, except for those of Edgar Snow, and perhaps Teddy White and Annalee Jacoby, I don't think they made much impact. Except for the comparatively small group with a great interest in China, I doubt that many people ever heard of Jack Belden, Graham Peck, or Agnes Smedley, much less Israel Epstein, good as their books were. There is a certain amount of intellectual incest among people deeply involved in their subject—in this case China—which inclines them to attribute more influence than really exists. And I have observed that the general public with some modicum of interest is more likely to read the reviews than the books, especially members of book clubs. (It would be interesting to see a comparative study of book sales of Belden, Snow, etc.)

The question arises, shouldn't the gatekeepers have tried to educate their readers? But the gatekeepers didn't know much more about China than their readers did, and the press is a money-making enterprise which, like any other competitive business, has to give the public what it wants. Would more copy have stimulated more interest which would have stimulated more copy? Which came first, as a comic strip asked recently, televised football or the six-pack?

An example given by Harrison Salisbury illustrated the importance that editors "back home" gave to stories with entertainment value.

I was part editor for the UP, and Walt Rundle was the originator of the egg story. It was based on the Chinese superstition that an egg will stand on end on New Year's Day. Rundle wrote the story and I seized upon it as *the* China story. It got more play than all the great political things that ever occurred. We couldn't wait for the next year to have the next China egg story.

It just was an example of the emphasis in news from China. This idiotic piece could capture headlines and play in every paper that you could imagine. Rundle got more congratulations for that story than I think all the other correspondents in China. This gives you some notion of the seriousness and purpose of American journalism!

Protesting the tone of Salisbury's comments, Peggy Parker Hlavacek defended the practice of focusing on human interest stories.

I arrived late in the game, and there were no restrictions on us at the end of 1946. I wrote lively stuff for the noisy *New York Daily News* because they paid well. I had to survive from one day to another, so I didn't travel, I didn't get around. But I think that what I wrote was perhaps what people wanted to read. That was what editors moved over the desk. And I dare suggest that the egg standing on end would amuse us even today. Occasionally in the pages of the *Wall Street Journal,* for example, you read a story about a cat or a new dog food or something, and it enlivens and illuminates the heavy stuff.

Mac Fisher:

I filed a story of an armored train attacking Peking. I was there and saw it and filed fairly copiously on it, as did

Jimmy White. After about six hours I got back a cable from New York via London, saying "File only world shakers. Shake in ten words or less."

Harrison Salisbury:

The editing problem certainly has existed from the very earliest times, and it has affected and always affects correspondents wherever they are. I've been a correspondent enough so I can say this with passion: It affects their product adversely. Editors always fail to understand the significance of the stories that the correspondents send in. They invariably undervalue these and send them the wrong kinds of messages, although I think the one that Al Ravenholt quoted, which I sent to him in 1945, was a pretty good message, because I believed at that time that the Russians were getting ready to come into the war against Japan, which they did right after we exploded our atom bomb. I was with the UP in this period, and the UP, as I'm sure you all know, was a very competitive news organization. It liked young people, which was one reason why so many people around here worked for it. It liked them and it paid them hardly anything, but it paid off with congratulations. You worked for $15 a week, but you might get five cables in a week saying that you'd done a great job. You'd just better not ask for a raise.

The UP was also interested in China, and this was a favorable circumstance. Why it was interested in China, I don't know specifically, but I think that Roy Howard, who founded the organization, had a romantic interest. And Carl Bickel, who was the great statesman of the UP in this period and who knew China, valued it very highly and was always interested in Chinese news, more seriously than many of the correspondents. He was interested in the Institute of Pacific Relations and, as a very young correspondent, he sent me out there to cover one of the Institute meetings, at which I first met a young Henry Luce, his father, and his wife.

I went back and looked up only the other day to see what the *New York Times* did on the great famine north of the Yellow River, in 1929 I believe it was, which introduced Ed Snow to the reality of China. There was only one story, one dispatch out of China carried by the *New York Times* on this famine, in which I believe at least six million people died. It was inside on page 12 and it read about six paragraphs. That was all six million people were worth to the *New York Times*, and you can imagine how little was published by other newspapers at the time. A few other items were published, appeals by American missionaries who came back from China and tried to raise money for the famine, printed some place back near the truss ads. So the judgment of editors in general, whether they worked for the agency that I represented or even the great *New York Times*, was not very sound as to what was really important about China and what was not. I give great credit to correspondents who were able in some fashion to dramatize the news that they were covering in such a fashion that they were able to get over the barricades of the editors.

Cost was a factor. We're not supposed to think of cost when we think about news, but China was distant, and unless you sent your dispatches back by mail or some of the extremely cheap cable and deferred wireless, it prevented many American publications and many editors from commissioning much from the field. And the agencies, particularly a cheapskate one like UP, very severely restricted the amount of news that would come in. You go back over the papers of the 1930s, and even the 1940s after the war started, and you'd be amazed at the small amount of genuine cable dispatch. And, of course, my job and that of several of my colleagues in New York was to take those three lines we permitted Ravenholt to send and expand them into a column of news by using our imagination and a few reference works. So there were all kinds of physical, economic, social, even cultural barriers to getting this news through.

On the other side, there was a feeling that news from China was more interesting than news from other places. If you were to try and calibrate the news from different areas of the world, then China would run pretty well, way ahead of news, say, from Japan. As for news from Southeast Asia, in those days there was none; India, practically none; the Middle East, none; Africa, none. All these were just blank spots, even in the *New York Times*. China rated pretty high, but not as high as Paris and London and Moscow, which had captured the fancy of the Americans when the 1917 revolution was over.

As we analyze the work of a correspondent in the field, we must keep in mind the things that he had to keep in his mind: How can I get the story to the editor? How can I get him to pay attention to it? Will he let me file another story on the subject? Those are very real questions. I'm sure it wasn't much different on the *Times*, the *Herald Tribune* (which paid a little better), and other great newspapers, and certainly about the same for the AP, except we always figured they had three times as much money. Here again, I should mention the influence that was mentioned earlier: the UP was strongly influenced by the University of Missouri. So many UP executives and correspondents came out of that school, and they all had an interest in China news. This played into the picture. I think somewhat the same thing was true of the AP.

Mort Rozanski, a historian:

Just to reinforce some points. One, the cost of cables. There's the trans-Atlantic cable and the trans-Pacific cable. Unfortunately, the trans-Pacific cable was 60 percent owned by the company that owned the trans-Atlantic cable. This was a hidden factor for many years. The consequence was that the cost of sending cable per word on the trans-Atlantic was 6¢ to 9¢ going into the early 1930s, and the cost of sending that same piece across the Pacific was anywhere from 30¢ to 90¢. And for urgent, it was $1.48.

That's one point. A second point concerns the cable as a restrictive element. In 1938 E. H. Houser was interviewed about this whole issue of the cables and was asked if that wasn't the major reason why the news wasn't getting to the United States, because the editors were concerned about cost. He came back strongly, saying that even if the cable had cost zero cents, he didn't think that it would be any different, because there simply wasn't that kind of an interest in China, period. And he could say that from personal experience.

A third point. From 1927 to 1931 and then again for a period in the mid-1930s, I conducted a survey of thirteen newspapers across the country. It indicated that China news stories were given greatest play in the *New York Times*. Overall they figured from number seven to nine in importance or depth of coverage compared to stories about other nations in the world.

The last point is about an editor, Nicholas Roosevelt, who was dominant for a while with the *New York Times* as an editorial writer. He came out to China in 1925, and he wanted to get more news about China into the *New York Times*. He wrote a letter to Nelson T. Johnson, who was of course very much involved in Far Eastern policy (he was minister to China for many years), about how more news about China could be gotten into the *New York Times* and particularly into the editorial pages.

They exchanged some information. In the end Nicholas Roosevelt wrote to Johnson and complained that in many cases the news coming back from China was so confusing and biased that the *New York Times* couldn't make up its mind whether it was leaning to the left or the right. Johnson wrote back saying that the problem of China was that there was a revolution going on and Americans simply didn't understand revolutions. They sought a quick fix, and unless the quick fix was there, they lost interest.

John Hersey then provided a graphic illustration of the difficulties encountered by the journalist trying to get a story into print and the ultimate effect upon the final product seen by the reader.

I want to get at the mind set, as it has been called, in this country toward China and toward Russia and the way in which I think it has been affected by the journalistic process. By process I mean the machinery that lies between the reporter's word in the field and the eye of the reader of the finished product. Let me take the *Time* process as an example. This may be more horrendous than some others, but I think you'll find analogies in the wire services and newspapers and other magazines.

Let's take it first from the end of the reporter in the field. In the Broadway Mansions (in Shanghai) your correspondent gets a cable from New York: "Recable soonest, takeout, famine, Sinkiang, Kansu provinces. Unspare colorful horrendous details." In New York they have no idea where Kansu is. So the reporter scrambles around and finally manages to get transportation, goes to the field, sees things which bring him to the verge of a nervous breakdown, gets back somehow to Shanghai, writes 6,000 words, sends them off, and gets drunk for three weeks.

Now let's look at it from the New York end. On Monday morning in story conference, the senior foreign news editor has seen a clipping on page 29 of the *New York Times* saying there are reports of a serious famine in the northwest of China and he says, "Well, I think we'd better have a story about this." So off through the news bureau goes the cable to the correspondent in Shanghai. By the following Sunday the cable has not come back from Shanghai and there is an agreement to postpone the story for a week. But even on the following Sunday the cable hasn't arrived from China and the senior foreign newswriter decides he'd better go ahead with the story anyhow. By this time there has been an accumulation of clips from the *New York Times*, the *Tribune*, Chicago papers, and the wire services on reports of this famine which have come from returned travelers, somebody from the Swiss embassy was up there and so on. The newswriter writes the story and then goes to see the foreign news editor, who puts in some fine touches and then it goes to the managing editor. The checker and the writer begin arguing about the accuracy of this story when finally the cable comes from Shanghai. And the writer reads it and says, "it-shay," and goes in to the managing editor and says we've got to fix the story, and the managing editor says put some stuff in, and he puts in five or six details from the cabled story.

And on the following Thursday the reader has twenty lines about one of the most terrible events in Chinese history.

This distortion process took place, of course, not only in China. In Moscow, when the controversy about Whittaker Chambers was going on, I received two small overseas editions of *Time*, got out my cables for the two-week period that were sent in response to queries from New York, and found that I'd sent about 10,000 words of material for these two issues. And I found in the stories, I can't remember an exact number, but something like 128 words which might conceivably have come from my cables, but might also have come from the *New York Times*, the *Herald Tribune*, or the wire services. (One of the cables I sent in was, "You're wasting money, bring me home.") But there were differences, and these differences had to do with the combination of this process with the personalities involved. I don't think you can disregard the personalities. They were, with respect to China, Teddy White, Henry Luce, Whittaker Chambers. Their temperaments, their mind sets, had an effect on what happened. The wonder was that much of the reality of the world did somehow come through.

But I want to get at the differences between this process in China and in Russia. Arch Steele was talking about the polyglot China correspondents group. There was no polyglot group in Moscow. We heard how Arch Steele, Till Durdin, and Al Ravenholt all got on various leaky vessels and drifted to China and got into journalism. In the 1930s and 1940s people didn't drift to the Soviet Union. You had to have brassbound credentials and there was a very, very set journalistic community. In China there was relatively free movement. If you w⁀ᴗted to get up to Kansu, you went to Don Kight and he cut you some

American reporters in Chungking, 1944, in front of the Press Hostel. Includes John W. (Bill) Powell, *directly in the middle of photo*; Annalee Jacoby Fadiman, *far right*; A. T. Steele, Jr., *fifth from left at top*; Albert Ravenholt, *far right at top*; T. H. (Teddy) White, *first row on left*; and Brooks Atkinson, *fourth from left at top*.   Courtesy of Arizona State University, A. T. Steele, Jr., Collection.

Veteran journalists and diplomats at the Scottsdale meeting, 1982. *Bottom row, from left:* Don Kight, James White, Harold Levine, John Hlavacek, Frederick Marquardt, and Mary Sullivan; *middle row, from left:* Peggy Durdin, Kay Lieberman, Marjorie Ravenholt, John Service, Caroline Service, and Walter Sullivan; *top row, from left:* Hugh Deane, Israel Epstein, Tillman Durdin, Harrison Salisbury, Julian Schuman, John Hersey, Sylvia Powell, John Melby, Ruth Potter, Phil Potter, Bill Powell, Albert Ravenholt, Hank Lieberman, Doak Barnett, John Fairbank, Annalee Jacoby Fadiman, Dorothy Borg, Wilma Fairbank, A. T. Steele, Jr., and McCracken (Mac) Fisher. Photo by Suzanne Starr, *Scottsdale Progress.*

Israel Epstein, 1982.   Photo by Suzanne Starr, *Scottsdale Progress.*

Peggy Durdin, 1982.   Photo by Suzanne Starr, *Scottsdale Progress.*

John Service, 1982.   Photo by Suzanne Starr, *Scottsdale Progress.*

Annalee Jacoby Fadiman, 1982.   Photo by Suzanne Starr, *Scottsdale Progress.*

A. T. Steele, Jr., 1982. Photo by Suzanne Starr, *Scottsdale Progress.*

Jack Belden, 1972. Courtesy of Sol Adler.

Hankow dinner party in August 1938. *From left:* Agnes Smedley, Frank Dorn, F. McCracken Fisher, Jack Belden, A. T. Steele, Evans Carlson, Freda Utley, Chang Hanfu, John P. Davies. Courtesy of John P Davies.

Hugh Deane, Jack Belden, and Israel Epstein in 1941 on the balcony of the Chungking Press Hostel. Courtesy of Hugh Deane.

Chou En-lai assistant Kung P'eng (right) and Ch'iao Kuan-hua in 1941 wedding picture. Courtesy of John K. Fairbank.

McCracken (Mac) Fisher and Liu Tsun-ch'i addressing staff at OWI office in Chungking, probably September 1944. Courtesy of McCracken Fisher.

General Claire Chennault meets the press on July 20, 1944, in Chungking. *From left:* Brooks Atkinson, unknown, Theodore White, Clyde Farnsworth, Bill Powell, Major Hyler, Jim Burke, unknown. Courtesy of Bill Powell.

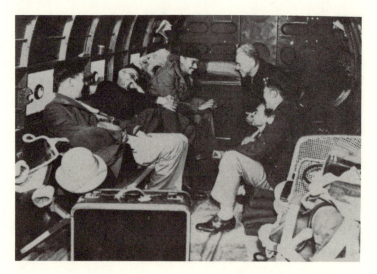

General Stilwell and the press, 1944. *From left:* Robert Martin, Stilwell, Brooks Atkinson, General Bergin, Theodore White (on floor), and Norman Song. Photo by Robert Bryant.

orders and you got there. Correspondents did go to Yenan. I went to Kalgan by borrowing the jeep from the American team in Peking and going up to the railhead, then getting on a flat car and riding up there unannounced. There was not this sort of mobility in Moscow. And let me illustrate that with an example of one story that *Time* really wanted.

There was this Dr. Frumkin—that really was his name. He was a plastic surgeon who had devised a surgical technique for attaching the penises of dead Russian soldiers to living soldiers who had had them shot away in battle. The remarkable thing about these devices was that after a certain period of recuperation, they would erect. This was a lot better story than an egg that only stood up on New Year's. They really wanted that story. So your correspondent could go to a Soviet official and say we would like to talk to Dr. Frumkin. The difficulty is that Dr. Frumkin works in a military hospital. The answer is, "Nyet." You write to the chief of the bureau, "Nyet." You write a letter to Molotov, no answer. You write a letter to Stalin, he doesn't answer. Then because you can persuade Ambassador Harriman that you will write a story that he wants written, he agrees to intervene and you may get to see Dr. Frumkin. I don't want to run it into the ground, but the environment was quite different from that in China.

There was no mobility in the Soviet Union. We were, in fact, incarcerated in the Metropol Hotel. It wasn't until the 1950s that you could even sneak up to the inner chamber and listen over somebody's shoulder. This kind of difference in the process had a very serious effect on the differences of perception that came from these two places. These differences did produce significantly different impressions in the public mind with respect to China and the Soviet Union. I think that the general public developed a sense that China was much more open to the possibility of pain, much more open to hope, than the mind set that developed with respect to the Soviet Union.

James White, recounting his role for more than a decade in covering and interpreting the China scene, illustrated the frequent shifts in editorial policy and the difficulties in presenting China news to the American public.

I had taken over the AP in Peking only a little more than a year before the Japanese struck at Marco Polo Bridge in 1937. From then until Pearl Harbor Day in December 1941, my assignment was to report from a vast occupied territory that ranged from the Yellow River to the Siberian border.

On Pearl Harbor Day I was temporarily in Shanghai, filling in for Clark Lee, who had been sent to Manila. The Allied community in Shanghai was too big for the Japanese to intern immediately, so I spent the next six months working for an American relief committee and moving heaven and earth to get my wife back from Manila where she'd been caught on her way home and interned at Santo Tomas. Jennifer got back to Shanghai in June, and we were repatriated on the first *Gripsholm* in the summer of 1942. After some weeks of rest and a family visit in California, we were assigned by the AP to its Washington, D.C., bureau, where I ran into many of the same people in the State Department whom I had known in Peking. The mutual confidences and help continued.

There were China angles to work on. I remember one press conference with T. V. Soong at the Chinese embassy when he had come on one of his pilgrimages to seek more American aid. He was putting out the standard line about how Free China was fighting on and on, getting the standard questions and giving the standard answers, so I tried a shot in the dark. Had the Chungking government, I asked, ever had a peace offer from the Japanese? T. V. looked startled, then he seemed to realize the opening he had been given. "Many times," he replied quietly.

After Germany surrendered in the spring of 1945 and the American war effort turned full-blast to the Pacific, the AP transferred us in July to San Francisco, where it was building up its Pacific cable desk to handle the enormously increased volume of news from the wind-up of the war and its aftermath. UP made comparable adjustments.

But in my case the AP assigned me to do a daily interpretive column on foreign affairs (which I argued against, because of the lack of sources, but finally agreed to try). This went on for a year and a half, until New York decided Europe was more important than that mess developing in China and took the column back.

It was another strenuous learning experience, with a regime of getting up at 4:00 A.M. to read uncut reports from the Orient and write an interpretive piece in time to make East Coast deadlines. Until commercial radio communications were reestablished we got piles of copy via military communications. After that ended we had regular Morsecasts from the main contributing bureaus like Tokyo, Shanghai, Manila, and Hong Kong, which enabled correspondents to file unprecedented amounts of copy. The AP even set up its own listening post in the East Bay hills and picked up the first faint signals from the Chinese Communist headquarters at Yenan, including John Roderick's dispatches.

The point of all this was that with such a volume and variety of news, even sometimes through censorship, you could, by paying close attention, tell what was going on. Also helpful were the still longer dispatches used in local papers from such feature services as the *New York Times*,

New York Herald Tribune, Chicago Daily News, Baltimore Sun, and *Christian Science Monitor.* Often full of useful background detail, these stories were used in full by subscribing papers.

Even after New York mercifully relieved me of the daily column, I kept careful files on Far Eastern developments and put together interpretive features through the years. Both AP and UP had excellent correspondents in China during the Civil War, and their uncut dispatches were far more revealing than what usually appeared in member papers. With the greater latitude allowed an interpretive writer, I was able to identify and analyze developing power struggles and point toward the probable outcome. Easiest, of course, was the Chinese Civil War, where the priority on both sides centered on survival and triumph rather than compromise and peace. Two years before the Communists took over in China I had written that they stood to win by default unless Chiang Kai-shek mended his ways.

Late in 1948 the AP finally decided to send me back to China to help cover the impending takeover by the Communists. But the new regime established in Peking never replied to requests for permission to go north, and I never got closer than Shanghai and Nanking. I visited Canton, Hong Kong, and Taipei, then flew home from Shanghai in March 1949. All this provided continuous contact with a wide variety of news from China during the 1940s and beyond, and is the basis for my judgment that on the whole the reporting from China was surprisingly good.

The climate this news encountered in the United States was confused by already developing Cold War tensions, frustration over the "loss" of China (just whom did China belong to?), and partly subconscious American prejudices rooted in fear, ignorance, and even racism.

Also, the nature of the American information media themselves and their treatment of foreign news added to the confusion. At every step, news from abroad has to compete with domestic news. The metropolitan dailies usually have enough space to give foreign news something of the lineage its importance deserves, and besides, when they have gone to the expense of sending their own correspondents abroad, they are less likely to cut what the correspondents send back. But most Americans rarely see a metropolitan daily, certainly not on a regular basis. They rely instead on their own local dailies, which rely on the news agencies, which for prevailing economic reasons "give them what they want." "What they want" too often turns out to be stories that are not too long to disturb the customary fare of local news, something similar to what basically is the headline service provided (with some notable exceptions) by the electronic media.

Other factors operate against the use of foreign news in American newspapers. One example: There is a widespread practice of seeking always to write news stories to conform with the "pyramid" theory of how to organize facts. That is, the main fact is in the lead, and other facts supporting or explaining the main idea follow in succeeding paragraphs in a descending order of importance. The theory is that a story so organized can be chopped off at almost any point and still make sense. Sometimes this works, but too often the makeup editor (whose ancestors probably dreamed up the theory in the first place) finds his space cramped and cuts too deeply. Stark facts are printed without adequate explanation of what they mean or imply. Meanwhile the big local story gets full play.

Headlining was another part of the gatekeepers' role. When the slanting of headlines by editors, which contra-

dicted or stretched the dispatches of China newsmen, was criticized, Henry Lieberman objected that the charge was unfair. Headlines are necessarily brief, he said, and no one can get the gist of a story into nineteen words, so no inference of tendentiousness can be drawn in most cases. Israel Epstein countered with samples from the New York Times (Lieberman's paper) for 1946 which he thought showed definite and misleading bias. Here are three examples with Epstein's comments.

> April 26: CHINESE LEADER OPENLY PROCLAIMS CIVIL WAR IN MANCHURIA
> This was written over a Durdin dispatch that did not state any such charge or place one-sided blame (the leader was Chou En-lai).
> April 26: CHINESE REDS BALK AT MANCHU PARLEY
> This story describes Chou En-lai as saying that a cease-fire should precede KMT-Communist talks on the Manchurian area, a condition by one of the parties, not a "balk."
> April 27: CHIANG SEEKS END TO MANCHU STRIFE
> This story indeed quotes Chiang, the other party to the fighting and to possible talks. A day earlier, Chou En-lai, proposing a cease-fire, had "balked" in the headline. Chiang, on the contrary, is taken at his word and even helped by the head over this story.

One could quote many more instances. But these may be enough to show that the headlines *were* slanted and did not reflect the dispatches or the situation.

Moreover, the news agencies were not entirely innocent of the practice of altering reports from the field, or adding material that changed the overall import of the story. Mac Fisher reported on experiences that occurred when he was United Press bureau chief in Hankow.

When I was stationed in Hankow in 1938 to report the Japanese drive toward and capture of that city, a number of my cables suffered "sea-change" before appearing in US papers. For instance, when I reported the departure of the American ambassador, Nelson T. Johnson, and his staff for Chungking, UP's version distributed in the United States and internationally said that "the Ambassador fled the beleaguered city for Chungking, the provisional capital of China." Actually, the ambassador and a skeleton embassy staff had simply followed the Chinese government and its offices to the new temporary capital of Chungking. As the ambassador pointed out to me in a pained letter of remonstrance, his duty was to keep close to the Chinese government, as I well knew.

This "pepping up" of my dispatch by the UP cable desk in New York understandably soured the ambassador's attitude toward the United Press for some time. Happily this distrust did not extend to me personally. I had long been on terms of mutual trust and confidence with him and members of the embassy staff, and they accepted my explanation of what had happened.

Other instances occurred during the same period. My parents had clipped stories in the Detroit papers of the Japanese advance on Hankow, "by-liners" credited to me. When I saw these on my return to the United States early in 1939, I was amazed (and distressed) to find that, into some of those I could recall, passages from the Japanese Domei News Agency had been inserted—with no identification as to source. Miles Vaughn, one of the editors then on the UP cable desk in New York, had long been bureau manager for UP in Tokyo and was regarded by colleagues as "pro-Japanese," which may account for these additions to my reports.

Finally, there was a more blatantly political form of gatekeeping, representing overt efforts on the part of em-

*ployers to modify their journalists' reports. Such prac-
tices became especially common with stories dealing
with the Kuomintang and the Chinese Communists. The
Time-Life organization under Henry Luce probably indulged in this more than most organizations. Annalee
Jacoby, an alumna of* Time, *supported John Hersey's observations on this point.*

On *Time* and *Life* we weren't concerned about cable
bills. Henry Luce was profligate. But when the news
reached New York, Whittaker Chambers received it. He
was foreign news editor, as John Hersey said, and his anti-
Communist prejudices either changed the story altogether or killed it. I had an interview with Chiang Kai-
shek once, an innocuous little interview. In the course of
it, I asked him whether he intended to return to Nanking
after the end of the war and he said, "No." He thought
the new capital might be Sian. This seemed such an un-
likely choice for a capital, lacking in communication or
space or buildings, that I sent the interview through and,
of course, it was not censored by the Chinese. Over the
hump the next week came *Time* magazine with several
pages of an interview full of questions I did not ask and
with answers Chiang Kai-shek did not give. A massively
anti-Communist diatribe, anti-Communist stories which
were not true, which none of us had ever heard of. I would
never have asked those questions. And Chiang Kai-shek,
in spite of his hatred of Communists, would never have
given those answers. Whittaker Chambers had sat in New
York and made up dialogue to put in the mouth of the
head of one of our allies.

*Marjorie Ravenholt also spent some time with the
Luce organization.*

In February 1946 General McClure, who was commander of the residual forces after Wedemeyer left, arranged for me to interview General Okamura. He was the Japanese general who was still operating out of Nanking and who commanded 150,000 Japanese forces whose purpose it was to hold all railheads in strategic points until the Kuomintang forces could gather themselves to take over, rather than let the Communists do it. I'm not sure why General McClure did this, because it made the Nationalists look very weak indeed. But they threw the story out of *Life* magazine in place of a story on some kind of scandal at home. They didn't even use the story, except to take a paragraph out of it and put it in *Time* to fortify a point that they were making about the strength of the Kuomintang. Completely turned it around.

Some correspondents noted that such overt editorial intervention was almost unique to Luce's organization. Al Ravenholt's stories, for example, were not subjected to such massive rewrites.

I think Harrison Salisbury will bear out the fact that those of us who worked for the United Press or the *Chicago Daily News* foreign services, the *New York Times*, the Universities Field Staff International, did not have this kind of copy problem generally. Sometimes they chopped off the bottom part of the story if they didn't have space. Or didn't use it. But I would say that in general we did not have this kind of editorial mishmash going on at headquarters.

Salisbury agreed.

Certainly the economic construction of the UP often caused us to take a 50-word item and expand it to a 400-

word item by adding background, and the result was not always what the purist would want. I don't think, however, that we even thought of injecting an editorial viewpoint into what we were writing. So far as the *New York Times* was concerned, during all the years that I wrote for them, the rule was (and still is) that there should be no change in a correspondent's copy without consulting the correspondent. Now this occasionally is violated, and when it is, it's a full court matter between the correspondent and the desk. Certainly those things do arise. But basically I found when I shifted from the agency to reporting for the *Times* out of Moscow that my problem was not interference or anything else from New York, but total indifference. I'd file and file and file. In the UP I used to get a quick staccato of messages back, but for months I didn't know whether I was really working for the *Times*. I hadn't received any direction of any sort.

7 | The Missed Stories

Apart from censorship, gatekeepers' activities, and public ignorance and indifference, some stories of potentially great significance never reached American readers. The reason: they were never written. The causes varied. Sometimes correspondents failed to realize the significance of an event. Other incidents were so profoundly critical of key personalities that editors and publishers capitulated before the possibility of libel. A prime example was related by Annalee Jacoby Fadiman.

I have a favorite story that concerns the mission of Patrick Hurley and Donald Nelson to Chungking in early September 1944. The war in Europe was soon going to end, and many supplies were going to be available to the Chinese. So Hurley and Nelson, after a great deal of tough bargaining, accomplished some miracles. That was the only time I was ever quite sure what American foreign policy was toward China. It was to get the Communists and the Kuomintang working together and to bring the war to a quick end, with as much as possible of the fighting being done on the China mainland by the Chinese. Chiang Kai-shek, I think most reluctantly, had agreed to let some minimal Communist representation join his government and, more important, he had agreed to let General Stilwell head all Chinese forces. Chiang Kai-shek's Kuomintang troops and Communist troops were to be commanded by General Stilwell.

At that point Donald Nelson went home and left Hurley to negotiate by himself, and Hurley decided to give a banquet for all the people he was dealing with and asked me to help arrange it. He invited most of the Chinese cabinet and a great many generals. He wanted me to stand with him as far away from the door as possible so that when each Chinese dignitary entered the door they would have to come fifteen feet or so toward us and I could tell him very quickly who they were so that he could get them straight. I put on my battered evening gown with my army raincoat over it and walked through the rain to Hurley's house.

The banquet was a great success at the beginning. There was a long banquet table with General Hurley at one end, myself at the other, and about ten eminent Chinese on either side. T. V. Soong, I think, was on my right. It went very well until, toward the end, after some toasting, Patrick Hurley got to his feet and said, "And now the most important toast of all." We'd already toasted Franklin Roosevelt and Chiang Kai-shek. He said, "I would like to toast the most important person in the world, my tall, blonde goddess of a bride." We smiled indulgently, but he was looking at me. I was at my prime: five feet three and a dark brunette and about as far from a goddess as it's possible to get. But he went on talking about our children, the joy I'd given him in our long life together. He asked all of his friends gathered together to join him in a reminiscence of our wedding night and how we were the last couple to leave the dance floor because he was too embarrassed to take me back to our rooms until the orchestra left the ballroom. This went on for quite a few minutes. We were paralyzed. Everyone in the room realized that this man did not know where he was, did not know who any of us were, and the next morning he alone was going to represent the United States in negotiations with many of the people in that room that would affect the future of the Civil War, United States-Chinese relationships, all kinds of things. Everyone filtered out in an embarrassed way, and because of this lapse into premature senility in full view of most of the Chinese government, I think a lot of rather fearful things happened.

General Stilwell did not lead united Chinese troops. He was fired and sent back to the United States within a few weeks. General Hurley arranged to succeed Clarence Gauss and became ambassador to China. He began to think the people were plotting against him, and he ruined the careers of probably the most loyal, intelligent, expert foreign service the world has ever seen [a reference to American Foreign Service officers in China including Service and John P. Davies—ed.]. I think Hurley was largely responsible for the decision to let the Kuomintang troops accept the Japanese surrender and for American planes to fly those Kuomintang troops up to the center of the Communist territories.

General Wedemeyer came out to succeed Stilwell. We all had great hopes that he would do something. Clearly no one under Hurley in the embassy staff could send in a report saying, "Our boss has lost his mind, please send help." But Wedemeyer arrived and lived with Hurley for several months. They had loud, noisy quarrels, and so far as I've been able to find out, Wedemeyer never even told the War Department the condition of Hurley's mind. I thought I should tell you about it since Teddy White and I tried to write this and the publishers said that libel suits would make it absolutely impossible. We had to choose between putting the story in the book and publishing a book at all. But it had some importance at the time.

Sometimes stories were lost because they seemed too improbable to be true. Al Ravenholt recalled one such incident.

We did not always believe the diplomats. For example, when I went back to Chungking at the end of October 1945 to close the United Press Bureau, I was invited over to lunch with Ambassador Pat Hurley. We had been drinking for three hours before we had lunch, and he recited to me the number of people he was going to "get" in the State Department. I thought he was drunk. I didn't realize that Pat Hurley was going to come home and really devote himself to this vengeful purpose.[1]

In some cases important stories were "lost" because their significance was not recognized by someone in the chain of news transmission—from the reporter in the field to the editor behind the desk. Al Ravenholt also addressed this point.

I think, as I look back, our basic failure was in not better understanding rural China and rural Asia. Teddy White in 1943 was covering the famine in Honan. That same year, I was covering the famine in Bengal in Eastern India when about five million people died. We knew, but we didn't cover it, that about two million people starved to death in Vietnam that year. That was just one dimension of things happening in Asia that never really got anywhere in terms of news. I had the good fortune in the summer of 1941 to live with the late Dr. J. Lossing Buck in

Chengtu, China. He took me into the villages and began to make me aware of the fundamental importance of the Chinese peasant. But I don't think that we found any editors who were that interested in the fundamental problems of what was happening in rural China. We had difficulty enlisting their interest in other rural areas of Asia as well, and this has continued up until the present time. Since the establishment of the People's Republic of China I have found an appalling ignorance, even among scholars in this country, about the state of agriculture in China and in much of Asia. There is a tendency to view the world through urban spectacles that have little to do with the rural areas. We all tended to be urban-oriented, as were our editors.

Another lost story goes back to July of 1945, when Annalee Jacoby was the Time-Life bureau chief in Chungking. Annalee and I gave a dinner at the press hostel to which we invited a select group of senior members of the US military headquarters in Chungking: General Paul Caraway, General Olmsted, and several others whom we considered exceptionally able. The question we put on the table that evening was, "What will be the most important decisions that the United States will make when Japan surrenders?" We ended up all agreeing that the most important decision that the United States would make when Japan surrendered would be where, when, and how we would transport the ninety-seven Chinese Nationalist divisions that had been trained by the United States in India and in South China under X Force, Y Force, and Z Force. This was the fundamental military setting for subsequent events in China.

That very issue prompted a meeting of the American commanders in Tokyo, immediately after the establishment of the American occupation of Japan. Admiral Barbey, who was commanding the Seventh Fleet, gave me the story of what happened at the meeting. The question was, "Where would we move the Nationalist troops to accept the Japanese surrender?" Barbey argued that we should only move them into the Yangtze Valley, that we should recognize that the Communists held the areas of North China, from the Yellow River north to the Great Wall. Of course, the Russians were accepting the Japanese surrender down to the Great Wall.

That story was never written, yet it was a story of what set the strategic basis for subsequent events in China during the Civil War. It denied the Communists the recognition they wanted. The decision was made by General MacArthur in Tokyo, and the State Department was involved to the extent that they enforced the edict that Japanese troops must surrender only to designated representatives of the Chinese Nationalist government. But this was what set up the strategic dominos for what became the Chinese Civil War. It was one of the major stories we missed.

Of all the China stories that didn't get reported during the 1940s, hindsight suggests one of the most pivotal was the offer in January 1945 by Mao Tse-tung and Chou En-lai to go to Washington to talk unofficially with President Roosevelt. They never got a reply. The incident was not mentioned at the Scottsdale conference.

The Mao offer was forwarded by the American Observer Mission in Yenan to the American embassy in Chungking, where it was stopped by Ambassador Patrick Hurley. He referred to it indirectly in a later message to Washington, but there is no indication that President Roosevelt ever learned of the Mao proposal.[2]

Another big story that was missed was that the Chi-

nese Communists were not as close to Moscow as was Chiang Kai-shek. Harrison Salisbury:

I want to raise one point on the question of important events that were not covered or were covered very furtively by China correspondents. It has to do with the split that emerged between the Communist party in China and that in Moscow. From almost the very beginning, Mao Tse-tung was on one line and Stalin was on another, and I think when you come up even into the 1930s, the united front period, there is a lack of understanding that this united front was blotting out Mao Tse-tung and the Chinese Communists, that the lines in Moscow were straight to Chiang Kai-shek and not to Mao. At least that's the way it seemed to me reading the dispatches. I'd like to know whether correspondents understood that and felt it, and what they felt during the war, when again the Moscow–Chiang Kai-shek alliance was in place, and when contrary to postwar impressions Mao and the Chinese Communists were isolated from Moscow to a major extent. This was not well covered. Maybe it couldn't have been, maybe it was too top secret. I don't know.

A question was raised by one of the historians concerning the correspondents' level of awareness of actions taking place in Communist-held areas. Specifically, to what extent were the journalists aware of the major party rectification (purge) or cheng feng *campaign of 1944, which was covered hardly at all by the American media?*[3] *Al Ravenholt replied.*

I was lucky because on the Yenan mission I had two close friends. One was Colonel David D. Barrett, the commander of the Dixie Mission. Dave and I had known each other since 1941. In the American army you had a number of individuals like Barrett who had had enough experience in China to know the score as well as anyone. I was also lucky because my friend, Dr. Melvin Casberg, was the doctor on the Dixie Mission. Casberg had come first to Kunming, where he decided he'd learn Chinese. He set up a free clinic for Chinese soldiers on the condition that every Chinese soldier would teach him one more word of Chinese. When General Stilwell sent the Dixie Mission to Yenan, he looked around for a doctor in the US Army who knew Chinese. Dr. Casberg was chosen, and because he was a doctor, he got around more than the rest of you did, if you'll forgive my saying so. He got around in odd places because he was treating people in the villages. He came back to me with a complete account of the *cheng feng* movement, very carefully documented. That movement simply got lost in the shuffle at the end of the war.

8 | Political Objectivity and Personal Judgments

"Missed" stories also could be attributed to political bias. In chapter 7 the question was raised in relation to gatekeepers. But how were reporters in the field affected by political bias? Or, putting it more bluntly: "Were the reporters biased in favor of the Chinese Communists?" as James Thomson asks in the Introduction. These are questions that did not occur to the reporters themselves because it was like asking, "Was I biased?" This was a generation of journalists in conscious pursuit of "objectivity" in what they wrote, so their initial answer at Scottsdale was, "No." Significant soul searching then followed, beginning with an illuminating discussion of the accuracy of reporting on the Kuomintang and Chiang's forces as compared to reports about the Communists and their armies. Henry Lieberman:

It was true in China that much of the criticism of the Kuomintang was based on the fact that a lot of our people were living in Kuomintang areas and could see what was going on. What was happening in Communist areas we didn't know anything about. I went to Yenan, as did others, and it was the Camelot of China to the outward eye. But it was also largely hidden from view, and much was unseen. We discovered a Russian presence in Yenan and were told, "Oh, those are Mao's doctors."

Also, when you got into areas where there had just been a battle you discovered that there were atrocities on both sides. Once when we were touring a battlefield under Nationalist auspices, it struck me that each fallen soldier seemed to have two wounds. One of them invariably was a shot in the head. It was amazing that there should be so many casualties with guys dying as a result of a shot in the head. It seemed clear to me that this was a case of Kuomintang atrocities. They didn't take any wounded. On the other hand, I came across one instance where someone was caught in a haystack and hacked to death. It was a Communist atrocity. The judgment to be made here is that when you get involved in a war some very unpretty things happen on both sides, and when you don't have full information you suspend final judgment but remain skeptical.

Peggy Durdin seconded the notion that "familiarity breeds contempt."

The idiocies, the mistakes, in the KMT area were pushed upon you every day. You knew the battles between the factions, you knew the miseries and all the rest of it. On the revolutionary side we knew very little and certainly not the seamier side of the factional fights.

Was the reporting of China biased because of the lack of hard knowledge about the Communists? Don Kight answered this question.

The implication, of course, is a bias toward the Left. Certainly there was a bias. Being human beings, newsmen have all sorts of biases. However—and this is the key point—despite their biases, the pressmen I knew made every effort to be utterly neutral and to report facts. Undoubtedly they were tripped up now and then, at least unconsciously, but they were a highly professional, capable group of reporters and no other group could have produced any better copy.

If bias crept in, it was probably on the side of the Gimo, and came from visiting reporters. Individuals or groups under the aegis of the War Department or some other agency were forever appearing on quick world trips. (A number of them were not first-class reporters, for the invited editor would turn his invitation over to some reporter as a reward for a local scoop.) These transients, inasmuch as they weren't very informed on China and couldn't ask embarrassing questions, were well received by the Chinese and granted interviews "my" correspondents had been trying to get for months, which used to drive me up the wall.

As to the quality of the reporting—remembering that there are always exceptions—the best estimate may come from a friend, a former newsman turned army public relations officer and now retired, to whom I sent a recently turned-up list of the reporters in China, without asking for any opinions. He wrote, "It gave me . . . a good feeling . . . to read down that roster and remember that there is such a thing as truly responsible reporting . . . one can at least look back upon and think about."

Phil Potter backed up Kight's remarks.

Were we reporters aware that the Chinese Communists were not agrarian democrats? Yes, we were, throughout. I was up in Kalgan, capital of a Communist border region government, and one thing that was pretty obvious to a newspaperman was the fact that in Communist China there was not a single newspaper other than their own party organ, whereas in Kuomintang China there was a comparatively free press. You had the *Ta Kung Pao* and you had many others, so that you got a sense of opposition to the Kuomintang government. A newsman could hardly be unaware of the fact that if you don't have a free press, then you're not an agrarian democrat.

What about the degree to which the assumed anti-Communist position of the American government might have influenced the slant given to stories from China? Did the correspondents consciously or unconsciously try to forestall anticipated criticism of their reports? John Fairbank:

On the origins of the Cold War and the function of the press in it, perhaps we could agree on a certain perspective. The folklore has been that the Cold War was forced upon us by the Soviets, but I think the conventional wisdom now among thoughtful people is that it came from both sides.

On the Chinese scene, we had, for example, the case of Pat Hurley and his plumping for Chiang Kai-shek when his staff wanted to remain neutral in a Chinese civil conflict. This was a premature example of the American Cold War attitude. A question in my mind is the degree to which American officials, and particularly army officers, were predisposed to assume that the American posture must be anti-Communist, since it had been that worldwide. In particular it had been anti-totalitarian against the Nazis, and weren't Communists totalitarian? There was a natural tendency to see the Cold War as a continuation of a just war against totalitarianism.

This general mind set, I rather assume, was in the American mentality and you found it in American officials and army officers. I think of Milton "Mary" Miles who was a leader in the anti-Communism cause very early. The joint US-KMT Sino-American Cooperative Organization (SACO) police headquarters and interrogation center in Happy Valley (near Chungking) is now a museum, with its torture chambers and evidence of American occupancy, and it's probably one of the must sights when you are in a tour group going to Chungking. Miles was a real boy scout with strong fascist proclivities. There must have been others like him scattered through the American establishment. When Walter Robertson became chargé after Hurley left (Walter was a Richmond banker) he knew what he thought about Communism.

The strategic posture against the Soviet Union came partly out of Washington. My question is, how much was anti-Communism in the blood and bone of the American establishment in China?

Bill Powell responded to Fairbank's query with an anecdote.

I think John Fairbank introduced a very important issue. Another side to it is the effect on the press of US government information and American officials attempting to sell their version of events to the press. We've all had experiences with that. If you're an American journalist working abroad you're really dependent on the consulate or the embassy. There's no way of getting around it. We have many examples where we've gotten pretty good information, but I'm sure all of us have examples where we were badly treated by our own government. Wedemeyer lied to me about the American troops in North China, for example. One time at a July 4th reception, Consul Davis, who was probably one of the ablest consul generals we ever had in Shanghai, took me aside and complained about an article I had carried. He said he didn't think it was a very good article. And I told him I thought it was quite a good article and said, "You know, if you'll point out to me anything with it that's wrong, why I would be very pleased." We went back and forth a little bit, and finally he looked at me. "Bill," he said, "the United States has its friends and it has its enemies. Its friends it looks after and its enemies have to look after themselves." This has always been the case.

Arch Steele:

In the time frame that John Fairbank refers to, anti-Communism was a very important element in our attitude, and it made it difficult to deal with the question of the Chinese Communists. Take for instance the visit of the correspondents to Yenan in 1944. I was not there, but I saw what they wrote when they came back. I talked to them and some of them were saying, "Well, these people are not Communists. They're promoting a new democracy up there," which they were. But it was only one stage on the road toward Communism. We were reluctant to paint them as real Communists, though, because we knew that that would go against the American grain. If you took a favorable attitude toward the Communists, it would probably have created, in the eyes of the publisher, a feeling that the correspondent in question was maybe pro-Communist. The mind set that we acquired in the United

States before we came to China predisposed us to take a position regarding Communism, and that affected to some extent our views and subsequently our dispatches on Chinese events.

In fact it made it very difficult sometimes to say favorable things about what we saw. But there they were. A trip from Chungking to Yenan was like going, in one sense of the term, from hell to heaven because everything in Yenan looked so orderly and the people were practicing democracy, or so they said, and to a large degree they were. And the Communists seemed to have found a formula that might open the way to a new day in China. But behind it all was this Cold War assumption that Communism was a monolithic structure and that the Chinese Communists, regardless of the differences in their behavior, were at heart totalitarian. And if you asked them, "Are you really Communists?" they'd say, "Of course, we're Communists." And they were. The new democracy was just a step in the direction of Communism.

Steele has stated clearly the problem of being politically "objective" about the situation in China in the mid-1940s. Increasing coverage of the corruption and unreliability of our ally Chiang Kai-shek coincided with positive reporting on the new democracy and effectiveness of the Communist-led guerrillas. At one level, as Steele points out, both kinds of news contradicted the growing cold war attitude at home. But at another level, negative coverage of Chiang Kai-shek and greater attention given to the Communists paralleled changing opinion within the State Department and among policy makers in Washington. As we shall see in the next chapter, the sacking of Stilwell in the fall of 1944 brought matters to a head, with policy conflicts in official Wash-

ington producing even greater contradictions in China reporting. We turn now to an examination of how closely the changing political objectivity, or bias, on the part of journalists in the field reflected or contributed to shifts at home in US government policy and public opinion about China.

9 | Press Coverage of China, American Government Policy, and Public Opinion

During the 1940s, basic American goals in China gradually shifted. From Pearl Harbor until V-J Day, the American government sought by every means to take the fullest possible advantage of China's geography, and to win the cooperation of China's manpower in a single-minded effort to defeat Japan. Although the Chinese government under the Kuomintang also wanted to see Japan defeated, its primary goal became that of surviving the challenge posed by the growing strength of the Communists. This difference in primary aims resulted in increasing tension between the United States and China. After the Japanese surrender on the USS **Missouri***, America's major interest in China was to see the emergence of a stable nation friendly to the United States. The chief aim of Chiang Kai-shek's government was to crush the developing "rebellion" led by the Communists. The strains brought on by these diverging basic purposes surfaced early with the recall of General Stilwell in late 1944.*

Earlier in a discussion of censorship (chapter 5) historian Schaller raised questions about why the American government temporarily relaxed restrictions on the press at the time of Stilwell's recall (October 1944). A plausible

157

interpretation is that Washington wished to use the press to put pressure on Chiang Kai-shek vis-à-vis its policy objective. According to this interpretation, Roosevelt agreed with Stilwell's view that the war should be expedited by means of a Chinese united front that was to include the Communists. To test this thesis, further examination of the Stilwell affair in terms of press coverage is needed as well as a search for other instances in which US government manipulation of the press occurred in pursuit of specific policy objectives.

We begin with historian Michael Schaller's comments on press coverage of the Stilwell recall.

The recall of General Joseph W. Stilwell by President Roosevelt in October 1944, most observers of Chinese-American relations agree, signified a turning point for both countries. In many ways, the event had as great an impact on China as did the Japanese attack on Pearl Harbor and the agreements emerging from the Yalta Conference. Yet each party derived a variety of contradictory lessons from the event. The Kuomintang leadership considered itself to have won veto power over an expanding American aid program and political commitment. For Roosevelt and then Truman, however, the crisis marked a turning away from their previous faith in and commitment to Chiang Kai-shek. Although neither president completely cut ties to the Nationalists, both administrations declined to grant much greater resources or support to a regime increasingly perceived as moribund, if not doomed.

The complexities of the Chinese-American alliance at least rivaled those of America's relations with its Soviet and British allies during World War II. As in those relationships, the problems of wartime censorship, secrecy, patriotic fervor, and simple lack of information often limited the ability of journalists to inform the public of problems in the alliance. The Stilwell recall raised the most fundamental questions of military strategy, coalition politics, civil conflict, attitudes toward revolution, and the clash of strong personalities. And all of these issues arose in the context of a national commitment to defeat Germany and Japan at all costs.

Given this jumble of complex, often contrasting, goals, how did major American newspapers and magazines present the command crisis in China and the issues surrounding Stilwell's recall? Did they, in fact, accept the glib official explanation that President Roosevelt offered the public, that the entire problem stemmed from a personality clash between Chiang and Stilwell? Or did newspapers and news magazines probe the crisis more deeply? How did the coverage of the Stilwell affair differ from previous reporting of the war in China and how did it affect subsequent coverage?

I selectively sampled only general interest periodicals, specifically avoiding scholarly journals such as *Far Eastern Survey* or *Amerasia*. I included *Time, Newsweek, Life, Saturday Evening Post, New York Times, Christian Science Monitor, The New Republic, The Nation,* and Associated Press dispatches in various newspapers. My sampling of press accounts, though admittedly impressionistic, suggests that coverage of the Stilwell recall represented a watershed in the presentation of Chinese political issues to the American public. A definite split emerged between "liberal" and "conservative" publications, but all accounts confirmed the existence of underlying political and military shoals upon which Chinese-American relations had begun to founder.

First a few points about depth of coverage, the problems of censorship having been raised earlier. The recall never appeared as the leading headline story in war reporting during early November when it became known. Not only did the naval battles around the Philippines receive greater play than the China crisis, but even relatively small battles in France and Belgium were given greater display in most daily newspapers. The story, even where covered, remained "hot" for only two or three days and then was dropped. China-based journalists who wrote postwar accounts (Theodore White, Harold Isaacs, Eric Sevareid) devoted far more attention to the events surrounding the recall than they were able to place in their parent publications during the war. Finally, in terms of volume of reporting, it is worth noting that far more stories were published during 1944 on the achievement of building the Ledo Road in Burma than on the recall of the commander in charge of building it.

The most comprehensive coverage appeared in the *New York Times,* beginning on October 28. On that day, a story by Bertram Hulen in Washington (*not* a lead story) declared, "Stilwell Moved from Orient at Request Laid to Chiang." Mostly a factual account of planned reorganization of the China-Burma-India Theater, it speculated that Chiang had demanded the removal after a conflict with Stilwell over troop deployments in the Burma campaign then underway. This story also cited an Associated Press report that a "high Chinese official" in the United States had attributed the recall to long-term personality clashes between the Generalissimo and the general. Again, it described the debate over Burma strategy as the catalyst.

Two days later, on October 30, the *Times* military specialist, Hanson W. Baldwin, reported on the issues "Behind the Recall of General Stilwell." Baldwin focused on the implications of the recall for pursuit of the war against

Japan. He dismissed rumors that personality conflicts explained the recall or that Stilwell would be reassigned to lead an invasion of the China coast. Baldwin suggested that internally China approached chaos, that the Nationalists faced opposition both from Communists on the left and from opportunistic warlords on the right. Corruption and military disintegration, he declared, had undermined the utility of the KMT armies. Stilwell had tried to remedy these problems, Baldwin wrote, by taking over the training, equipping, and command of the massive but disorganized Chinese forces. Hardly an idealist, Stilwell led a hard-nosed, well-informed effort to utilize Chinese manpower against Japan. Without explaining in detail the reasons for the KMT opposition, Baldwin suggested that the recall functionally rendered China a marginal part of the remaining war effort in the Pacific. This account demonstrated a fairly sophisticated and accurate description of the event.

The key *Times* story appeared on October 31, 1944. Brooks Atkinson wrote the account and hand-carried it out of China to avoid censorship. Though it appeared prominently on the first page, the story was not a top headline. Atkinson's report carried the lead, "Stilwell Break Stems from Chiang Refusal to Press War Fully." Not only was this one of the longest reports to be published, but it also retains a unique historical and literary immediacy forty years later. Atkinson described the three-year background of conflict between the American and Chinese commanders. By mid-October Chiang had apparently decided that getting rid of Stilwell represented his best hope of gaining control over Lend-Lease supplies and of preventing any US assistance to his Communist foes. Control over foreign aid and the conflict with the Communists, the story emphasized, underlay the crisis.

Atkinson portrayed Stilwell in almost heroic terms, describing him, with no irony intended, as a new "Chinese Gordon." He suffered defeat not at the hands of the ostensible enemy, Japan, but at the hands of America's presumed ally, Chiang. Not only would his recall render China a useless ally, Atkinson warned, but American acquiescence to Chiang signified "the political triumph of a moribund anti-democratic regime that is more concerned with maintaining its political supremacy than in driving the Japanese out of China. America is now committed at least passively to supporting a regime that has become increasingly unpopular and discredited in China, that maintains three secret police services and concentration camps for political prisoners, that stifles free speech and resists democratic forces." The "real" issue between Stilwell and Chiang, Atkinson concluded, was whether to pursue the war against Japan or to accumulate American aid for a civil war against the Communists. By dumping Stilwell, Washington had implicitly cast its vote for Chiang's strategy.

Atkinson's graphic account set the tone for almost all subsequent stories critical of the Kuomintang and American policy. An Associated Press report of November 1, by the agency's Chungking correspondent, Thoban Wiant, "China in Dictator's Grip," closely paralleled Atkinson's. In a significant oversight or misinterpretation, neither Atkinson nor Wiant understood Patrick Hurley's devious role. They miscast the presidential envoy as a devoted supporter of Stilwell (a misperception initially made by the American commander as well) who had labored desperately and in vain to convince Chiang to cooperate with the general. In fact, no full understanding of Hurley's role in the crisis emerged for some time.

The *New York Times* culminated its reporting of the crisis on November 2, 1944, with an editorial labeled

"China Crisis." In a very wishy-washy presentation, the editors accepted neither the accounts of Atkinson nor FDR's claim that no really important conflicts underlay the recall. The editorial stated the obvious truth—that something more than personality problems caused the break. But it insisted that Chiang Kai-shek must still be considered a major, valuable ally who must not be alienated by the United States. Hopeful of a compromise, the editorial urged continued American aid to the KMT regime, but called upon Chiang to be more flexible in accepting American advice and to consider utilizing the Communists against Japan.

Like the *Times,* the *Christian Science Monitor* carried several serious reports on the recall. Writing from Washington on October 21, Neal Stafford analyzed the recall as resulting from Stilwell's selfless effort to stem KMT corruption and reorganize nearly useless Chinese armies to fight against Japan. Unless the Communists were utilized, he explained, China could not become a serious factor in the anti-Japanese struggle. The *Monitor* noted that its reports were based on evidence gathered from other reporters since its regular correspondent, Guenther Stein, had been unable to send his stories through Chinese censorship.

On November 1, a second story by Stafford discussed FDR's press conference in which the president denied substantive problems with China. The *Monitor* reporter subtly refuted the president's denial and made plain his own belief that the problem of arming the Communists and cleaning out KMT corruption lay at the very heart of the Stilwell recall. Not personality but deep internal division within China and between Washington and Chungking explained the crisis.

A *Monitor* editorial page commentary by Joseph C.

Harsch, on November 2, repeated these themes. Harsch was one of the few journalists to discuss explicitly how censorship had shaped the reporting of events in China. The current relaxation of censorship, at least by American authorities, suggested that Washington hoped to use critical press coverage as a weapon against Chiang's regime. Harsch pointed to the KMT–Chinese Communist Party (CCP) confrontation as the very core of all American problems with the Nationalists. Chiang's determination to gain control of American aid supplies revealed his determination to bar Communist links to America and ensure sufficient weapons for a civil war. The Generalissimo had won the battle, but Harsch predicted that his image with the American government and public had been fatally tarnished.

Two liberal political weeklies, *The New Republic* and *The Nation*, weighed in heavily against the Chinese Nationalists when they reported the Stilwell recall early in November. *The Nation* repeated most of the praise of Stilwell and critique of Chiang found in the *New York Times* and Associated Press reports. Its November 4, 1944, issue described China as a useless military ally in the war and a questionable political partner in postwar Asia.

The New Republic, on November 6, also in an unsigned editorial, labeled the Stilwell recall a defeat for Chinese democracy. Stilwell represented as much a force for positive political change within China as a crusader for military action against Japan. Without him, Chiang would probably begin an internal campaign against rival warlords and the Communists. The editorial specifically denounced the Kuomintang regime as a reactionary, incompetent, and dubious ally.

Three mass circulation news magazines, *Newsweek*, *Time*, and *Life*, handled the issue rather differently. The first two relied on highly skilled professionals in China, Harold Isaacs and Theodore H. White, respectively. Isaacs' account appeared in the November 13, 1944, issue of *Newsweek*. The lead noted that Chinese censorship had tried to suppress the report, and the author had smuggled it out. The *Newsweek* story was fully as critical of the Chinese Nationalists as the Atkinson account. Stilwell's recall, Isaacs asserted, removed any chance China would play a part in the defeat of Japan. He concluded that American leaders, whether they publicly admitted it or not, had "written China out" of future military strategy. Stilwell's only guilt in the affair, Isaacs reported, lay in struggling to root out corruption, prevent civil war, and make China a real fighting force. Although Washington initially backed Stilwell, FDR ultimately "pulled the props from under the general and let Chiang have his way."

Isaacs placed the recall crisis in the perspective of the previous three years of tension in the Sino-American alliance. He explained how a succession of powerful emissaries had tried to prod Chiang into actively pursuing the war and to warn him against civil conflict. Isaacs, too, misinterpreted Hurley as a friend of Stilwell who led a last-ditch attempt to convince Chiang to grant him full authority. The central problem of lifting the blockade of Yenan and arming the CCP against Japan, Isaacs reported, overrode the issue of tactics in Burma, command over particular units, and the alleged arrogance of Stilwell.

Whatever Isaacs thought of Hurley's role in the recall, he did voice some doubts about the new envoy's glib efforts at solving the CCP-KMT standoff. Almost immediately upon the general's firing, Hurley began personal negotiations with Yenan and claimed a breakthrough. But, as the journalist cautioned, "Hurley, seemingly alone of all informed people, believes progress is being made.

Promises made in this deal can be taken as real only if and when they are actually carried out and that won't happen in a hurry." Following upon these central themes, on November 20, *Newsweek* published another story by Isaacs denouncing gross corruption among the KMT armies and exposing their blatant squandering of American assistance.

Time covered the recall in two stories. A brief notice appeared on October 30, 1944. Part of a general survey of world battlefronts, it was one of the few reports that stressed the personality clash between Stilwell and Chiang. Implicitly, it expressed approval of the recall and informed readers to take heart in the fact that Claire Chennault, "the hero of the people and the confidant of Chiang Kai-shek," remained on duty.

The major *Time* story appeared on November 13. Presumably based on reporting from Theodore White, it had a schizophrenic quality. The first section of the account examined the background to Stilwell's mission and larger reasons for his disagreements with Chiang. It disputed the claim that personality lay behind the break, and portrayed Stilwell as a skilled, forceful, dedicated, and informed commander. British war aims in Asia (which did not include helping China), Chinese domestic conflicts, and muddled American political interference were all listed as factors complicating his command. It also noted the efforts of Roosevelt and Stilwell to compel Chiang to make peace with the Communists, at least long enough to fight Japan. The report even admitted that, all else aside, Nationalist China must be considered a dictatorship bent foremost on pursuing a civil war against the CCP. At this point, the report quoted a lengthy passage of Brooks Atkinson's searing denunciation of the KMT.

Suddenly, in mid-stride, the *Time* report changed direction. It proceeded to denounce American supporters of the CCP as apologists for Red totalitarianism. It cited critical reports about Yenan from renegade Chinese Communists. The CCP, it charged, was largely responsible for subverting Chinese unity against Japan and had compelled the KMT to maintain the costly blockade of Yenan. "If Chiang relaxed the blockade, perhaps all of China would ultimately be lost to the democratic cause," the magazine argued. The story ended by severely chastising FDR for botching Asian policy by pressing Chiang to compromise with the Communists. Any coalition, it warned, would eventually result in a Red China allied to the Soviet Union and working against American interests in Asia.

Comparing the wildly inconsistent introduction and conclusion to this report, one must assume that either Henry Luce or those close to him, like Whittaker Chambers, rewrote and mangled White's reporting to justify Chiang's actions. This again raises the issue discussed earlier of how other editors may have slanted similar reporting elsewhere.

The effort to present the Stilwell recall as the opening act in an Asian cold war appeared in the other major Luce publication, *Life* magazine. In a major editorial of November 13, 1944, *Life* argued that the personality clash between the two principals was only a minor facet of a major problem. It considered American treatment of its ally and war strategy in the Pacific as far greater problems. Washington, it claimed, was truly to blame for China's failures on the battlefield by offering only scant and tardy aid. FDR had tried to pass the blame to Chiang by provoking the recall and allowing American censorship to pass stories unjustly critical of the KMT leader. In fact, *Life* charged, American journalists who supported Stilwell actually parroted Communist propaganda. The only problem with China's armies and commanders, the magazine boldly asserted, was a shortage of Lend-Lease weapons.

Not only Stilwell and his aides, but the American diplomatic service in China, came under *Life*'s harsh scrutiny. Ironically, the magazine attacked the best-informed diplomats as being wholly ignorant of Chinese culture, language, and history. This group (in a forewarning of postwar attacks) was blamed for failure to see that the CCP represented nothing but a Soviet proxy. Chiang, of course, fully understood the Red threat and deserved complete American support in suppressing it. In any case, what Chiang did with Lend-Lease and his armies was his own business, not Roosevelt's. The editorial concluded with a rousing declaration that the future of American interests in the Pacific rested on a strong, friendly China under Chiang's personal leadership.

Summing up, it seems clear that even those journals supporting the recall and the Nationalists' policies recognized some of the deeper issues. Virtually all lengthy accounts noted the three-year background to the crisis, its dire implications for military strategy in the Pacific, the effects it would have on future political cooperation with China, and the primacy of the KMT-CCP conflict to this and virtually all policy questions. Although the Luce publishing empire strongly backed Chiang and attacked the germ of Red subversion it found in Roosevelt's foreign policy, most working journalists and popular periodicals strongly supported Stilwell and criticized FDR for indulging a decadent Kuomintang. It seems clear that the press did manage to use the crisis to transmit to the American public an accurate vision of the immense struggle about to engulf China. Whether anyone knew how to interpret the evidence is quite another matter.

How was the evidence interpreted? Did press reports out of China—or the reporters themselves—have any effect on US China policy, or was the flow mostly the other way, with Washington manipulating journalists through censorship and other means? The correspondents tended to regard themselves as observers, recorders, reporters of events, not as participants or actors on history's stage. For instance, Don Kight, the army's press officer from 1944 to 1949, was of the opinion that the press had relatively little effect on policy makers or public opinion.

Did the news reported out of China and the books written about it reach and influence policy makers? I would judge that the material was devoured by second-level policy makers—say, the China Desk of the State Department. From subsequent events, I doubt that it reached the decision-making policy makers. There is little evidence that top-level policy makers involved in the Vietnam war had ever read, say, the State Department's "China White Paper," much less the works of Sun Tzu or Mao; otherwise we either would not have gotten into Vietnam or we would have fought a different war. Top-level policy makers are notorious for disregarding the advice of their experts when it doesn't agree with their preconceived notions. There are numerous instances of such disregard of intelligence data.

One correspondent [Steele] has commented on the lack of interest by policy makers in talking to him after he returned from China. The same lack of interest obtained on the part of the general public, in my experience. I visited relatives in a small town after my return. I was asked a couple of polite, perfunctory questions, and then the conversation turned to last night's poker game, the price of corn, or an item of gossip. Yet many of these people read the *Baltimore Sun*, which carried some of the best reporting on China (by Mark Watson and Phil Potter), and a number of them read the *Washington Post*. When I returned from Peking in 1950 after six months with the Communists, one would have thought my relatives and friends would be at least mildly interested, but I got the same perfunctory questions. People are interested in what affects them personally—and they weren't affected personally by China, so they didn't have much interest. In sum, then, I don't think the press had much influence.

Henry Lieberman concurred with Kight, elaborating further on the public's ignorance and naiveté about China.

I never had much confidence that I was having any impact at all on American policy. When I got back to the United States I was not surprised, and not bothered at all, that people were not knocking down my door to ask me what happened in China.

I arrived once on home leave while my mother was visiting with a neighbor. Alerted that I was home, she brought the neighbor with her. I was in full regalia, sun tan and all. The neighboring lady was a New Yorker and a reader of the *New York Times*, I'm sure. My mother said, "He just got back from China." She said, "Oh, isn't that nice. Did you drive?" This is the kind of thing that makes you humble.

The question of government manipulation of the press was raised at the outset. From time to time the press was the means by which Chinese officials tried to sway US policy—sometimes with signal success. But it was only possible if Chungking had Washington's tacit approval. This was the case in January 1942 when the State, War, and Treasury departments wanted quick congressional approval of a half-billion-dollar, no-strings-attached loan to China.[1] Mac Fisher, then United Press bureau chief in unoccupied China, recalled what happened:

Chungking in 1941 and 1942 was a buzzing beehive of rumor. Innumerable "sources" were willing to tell you exactly what was happening, and what was surely going to happen next. But no one would be quoted. Most of us felt that "it is learned from usually reliable sources" is not a persuasive lead to an important story.

At one point I became fairly sure that the many rumors to the effect that China was considering accepting one of the Japanese "peace offers" had some substance. I telephoned Sun Fo, son of Sun Yat-sen and then chairman of either the Legislative or the Executive Yuan, and asked for an interview. He agreed and asked me out to his home along the Chialing River. When I arrived his friend Quo Tai-chi, the foreign minister, was also there. Quo had frequently given me both "on the record" and "off the record, not to be used" material.

We discussed the question. Sun acknowledged that some consideration was being given to pulling out of the war. China had borne the full brunt of Japanese attack and aggression alone for five terrible years—ten including Manchuria. Resources were exhausted. Sun and Quo conferred and agreed that Sun could be quoted. Knowing that the censor would never pass such a story on my say-so, I asked if I could borrow a typewriter. I was shown to a small room, sat down, and typed out my proposed telegram. Sun and Quo read it. I do not recall that they asked for any changes. I then asked them to sign the original; we all three knew the text would be likely to produce near heart failure in Hollington Tong of the Information Ministry, chief censor of outgoing press copy. I took the telegram directly to Holly, who telephoned at least Sun and Quo to make sure he would not be held responsible if he let it go. I think he was as surprised as I that it was approved for release. Needless to say, immediately after sending the telegram I provided the embassy with a copy, and explained all the details of the interview and its clearance. A few days after publication of the interview in the United States, Congress voted a half-billion-dollar loan to China.

Congress, then, was more attentive to press reports than were the officials in the State Department. Nancy Tucker:

Lacking independent sources, apart from occasional trips and personal correspondence, and rarely privy to State Department information, congressmen had to rely upon journalists. In addition to culling factual data from the newspapers, congressmen and their assistants avidly read columns and editorials. James Reston, weighing the influence of newsmen on foreign policy, found that it was "exercised primarily through the Congress, which confuses press opinion with public opinion."[2]

Did some reporters play a more direct role in influencing US policy? A few acknowledged they had been "debriefed" by officials in Washington, that their views had been asked. Most had not. Arch Steele:

When I returned from the Orient I would usually take refuge in Boise, Idaho, capital of the potato state. Usually the State Department didn't even know that I was in the country. I was never sought out when I returned from China.

When pressed, however, memories produced a more complicated picture. Some reporters, at least, had been sought out by American officials. Till Durdin recalled:

The American newsmen were as a routine matter in touch with State Department people, Defense Department people, CIA people, anybody we could find who might be helpful in getting at information. When I was on home leave, the *Times* made provision for me, as it did with other correspondents, to visit Washington for a week and go see officials in my field of endeavor. So it was not a question of anyone seeking me out, I sought them out.

Once, however, when I was on home leave in Washington, the CIA called me up and said, "I wonder if you'd come around and be debriefed." I thought it was the patriotic thing to do, so I went around and was debriefed as to my views on China.

Arch Steele:

I'd like to amend my remark about not being sought out. Till's comments bring to mind one occasion when I was sought out. Not by diplomatic personnel, but by the Office of Strategic Services (OSS), who invited me to participate in a secret mission. I declined.

Al Ravenholt then related an anecdote illustrating the futility experienced by those who did advise the government.

In August 1950 I wrote two articles for the *Chicago Daily News* from Hong Kong on the Chinese Communists' military preparations to enter the Korean War. I then went to the Philippines to do some articles and arrived in Chicago in early September. I received a request from the White House to come to Washington. Livingston Merchant was the man who called me into the State Department. And the principal subject of discussion was, "How do we head this [China's entry into the Korean War] off?" See, at the time I had spelled out in some detail the military preparations the Chinese Communists had made, with the transfer of the new Fourth Field Army from South China into Manchuria. We touched on the fact that Hank Lieberman's and my mutual friend, Ambassador Pannikar of India, was hardly the most reliable channel for the US to be using to negotiate with the government in Peking. Then I was asked to come over to the White House to see Colonel Frank Roberts, who was in the office of the Chief of Staff, and we discussed what Hank, Till, Phil, and the rest of us had seen of Chinese Communist military capabilities. Colonel Roberts was a sanguine, sane, concerned person. As you know, he went with President Truman to Wake, where they tried to impress upon General MacArthur that the Chinese Communists were getting ready to come in. General MacArthur dismissed it, and the Chinese Communists crossed the Yalu on October 25, 1950, and drove us almost to the southern end of Korea. What I'm trying to say is that while we would occasionally be in this situation of providing information and providing the best of what we understood, that didn't mean that rational action resulted.

Robert Blum, an expert on US Asian policy in the late 1940s, recounted how Newsweek's *Harold Isaacs's advice on policy toward Bao Dai was ignored.*

I can give testimony to one contact of Harold Isaacs with the State Department. He was covering Indochina after the war, and was a very astute observer. He came back on several occasions and talked to a State Department press officer, Charlton Ogburn. Ogburn left a very good memorandum about an extensive conversation he had with Harold Isaacs back in late 1949 or early 1950. The drift of it was that the United States should not back Bao Dai, and that Bao Dai was not popular anywhere in Indochina and didn't have a chance. Isaacs wanted to see more senior people in the State Department, but they did not have time for him. He ended up speaking to Ogburn, a relatively junior State Department official.

Perhaps the most striking and blatant example of a government effort to influence the press and to justify American policy was the "China White Paper" of 1949 produced by State Department officials. John Melby, the principal compiler of the White Paper, had this to say about the mood of mid-level policy-makers in Washington during the late 1940s.

I was in the Nanking embassy from 1945 until 1948, and then I was stationed in the State Department in Washington. I think that the Department was following what was being reported in the press, but I'm afraid I also have to add that I think that what was being reported and the department's reaction to it really had little if any influence on the development of American policy. Nobody, but nobody, paid any attention to what the Foreign Service and the Department thought about China. I think you can make it just as simple as that.

Robert Blum:

When you think about the people who were making decisions on American foreign policy in East Asia, they were not exactly a *tabula rasa* on the subject. You had Walt Butterworth, who spent considerable time there and who had been in the Marshall mission. You had, before him, John Carter Vincent, who had served in China most of the time since 1924, finally becoming counselor (second in command) of the embassy in Chungking in 1941. They had views, definite views, on the way things were going. Dean Rusk had been there, and he had a lot of influence, probably a determining influence, on US policy. The man with the most open mind was Dean Acheson, and he was all over the lot in 1949 on different things that the US could do. When information came in, it was read and used for assessing policy to date, but it was a policy that had been in place for quite a while. And my impression is that people had basically made up their minds about which way things were going. Frequently people with very closed minds were some of the key actors in the Defense Department and elsewhere on the Hill.

Doak Barnett:

John, I'm surprised. I would have thought, to begin with, that the climate which produced the White Paper, which you, John Melby, had a great deal to do with, was almost certainly influenced by the general reporting, not only by diplomats but also by the press.[3] There were really two—probably more than two, but at least two—major competing streams in the policy debate that was going on. My judgment is that most of the press reporting, as well as most of the diplomatic reporting, was in the direction of accepting the change in China, accommodating to it, and moving toward recognition. This did have influence on policy, in my opinion. It was reflected not only in the White Paper, but also in the Truman-Acheson speeches made in January 1950. I think we were moving gradually in one direction as a result of the influence of not only diplomats but also the press.

The other competing influence was also very strong, especially among newspaper owners and publishers. As I said earlier, it came largely from major publishers in this country. It came from Luce and company. It came from those who ran the Hearst empire, and it came from those who ran Scripps Howard. They were working in exactly the opposite direction. Luce et al. were very ideological in their reaction to what was happening in China—very opposed to accommodating to what was happening, very opposed to recognition of the Chinese Communists, and so on.

One can only speculate about "what if," but my speculation is somewhat in line with what I think you're implying. If the Korean War had not occurred, I think that within a year or two we would have moved toward recognition and that the Chinese would have become more flexible over time. Without the Korean War, things would have been very different, in my opinion. But the Korean War did occur and certain policy decisions were made, very rapidly, without consideration of the long-term consequences.

This is where the opposite press influence—such as

Luce's—was very strong. A combination of major publishers plus key congressmen and the Defense Department were opposed to accommodation. This meant that Secretary of Defense Louis Johnson could go into Blair House the day after the attack on Korea and present a MacArthur memorandum urging the United States to intervene in Taiwan. Truman and Acheson decided, after almost no debate, and no consideration of the probable long-range consequences of reopening the question of Taiwan's legal status, to again involve the United States in the Chinese Civil War.

They were trying to get the military, plus Congress, to support what they felt was necessary in Korea. If the Korean War had not taken place, things would not have been the same. We didn't start the war and the Chinese didn't start it. We were both involved as a result of decisions others had made. If there had been no war, we probably would have had relations after a couple of years. If that had been the course of events, then one might have looked back and said that the reporting of diplomats from China, and also the reporting of the press, had laid the groundwork for accommodation to the new Chinese regime.

Gaddis Smith, a historian, amplified Barnett's statement by focusing on the role of journalists in the creation of the White Paper.

I'd like to make some remarks about the background of the White Paper and ask if John Melby would respond. The White Paper had several audiences in China and the United States, probably even in Moscow. But certainly one of its messages was that events in China are Chinese, to emphasize what Israel Epstein said earlier: the Chineseness of the situation. And maybe I have an overly romantic view of the relationship of the press and the diplomats in this period, but it seems to me that the China White Paper, which was government-sponsored journalism in a large sense, was the biggest single journalistic effort in the decade, and that it did reflect this symbiotic relationship, the close rapport between diplomats and journalists. It seems to me there was a consensus among many of the diplomats and the journalists, whose dispatches were selected in large measure by John Melby for inclusion in that document. I'd like to ask John if that's just a historian talking through his hat.

Melby responded:

There's a great deal to it. The origins of the White Paper came out of conversations between John Davies— he was then on the policy planning staff—and me when I got back from China early in 1949. We played around with the idea of writing a "Mr. X" article on China and finally came to the conclusion that China was too big a subject for that. Davies took the idea to the Secretary, Dean Acheson, who very much liked it and took it to the president. The president then issued a directive to the Department and, of course, indirectly to me because I was selected as the principal coordinator of the document, that we were to write the record and write it straight, no matter who was hurt. We were to put all the facts on the table and let the facts speak for themselves. And that is precisely what we did. The whole document, more than twelve hundred pages, was compiled in about five months and finally published in the first week of August 1949.

I would say just a couple of words about the unfortunate letter of transmittal, which is what most people read at the time. I did the first draft of the letter of transmittal.

The Paper then became very well known in the Department. The fact that we were compiling the thing had been kept fairly secret within the Department until I did that draft letter, whereupon everybody in the Department had to get in on the act. It read like every letter drafted by a committee of the whole, which is about what it was. Unfortunately, Mr. Acheson decided just to sign it as it was. I don't think he ever anticipated how many people would pick on this letter and attack the whole document because of the letter of transmittal. But that is what happened.

Our sources consisted primarily of reports in State Department files. We also went over War Department files as well as General Marshall's files. Phil Sprouse, who was also involved in it, was responsible for going over General Marshall's files. What I didn't know at the time was that Phil Sprouse had written General Marshall's report to the president; he had actually drafted Marshall's report. So he had access to the Marshall papers.

At least one journalist was consulted for advice about the document. Till Durdin:

My home leave from my post as *New York Times* correspondent in China was just about ending. I was going to pass through Washington on the way out and see a few people when I got a call from John Melby saying, "Why don't you come over and have a talk?" I came over and he said, "We've got this thing, the White Paper, and I wonder if you'd read it over and give us your views on it." I was due to leave and the *Times* expected me to take off the next morning for China, but I stalled them and spent several days reading this tome. I thought it was a great document and I said so. I said, "I really have no additions or emendations to make."

The ambiguity of Durdin's connection to the White Paper underlines the difficulty of assessing the direct influence correspondents may have had on America's China policy. But the reverse is much clearer. American government manipulation of the press in pursuit of specific policy objectives occurred regularly.[4] Censorship was lifted for policy reasons at the time of Stilwell's recall in 1944 as well as in 1942 when rapid passage through Congress of a 500-million-dollar loan to China was needed. The final proof lies in the biggest journalistic effort of the decade launched by the State Department in 1949, which produced the China White Paper. The White Paper illustrates how closely the government and the press had become intertwined in this period, with government usually leading the press rather than the other way around. Or, to put it more charitably as one of the veteran journalists did in Scottsdale: "The government's own venture into journalism in issuing the White Paper is sufficient acknowledgement of the importance policy-makers attached to this function of the press, and the close attention they paid to it."

Press influence on public opinion was another matter. Outside of influence on Congress, it is hard to pin-point. The daily press China reporters who gathered at Scottsdale did provide the public—and Congress—with a great share of the information upon which they based their opinions. On the other hand, public ignorance and disinterest in China and the Far East remained high. Shaping the digestion of information and formulation of snap judgments about China and US policy were many other influences, not the least of which were crusaders like publisher-editor Henry Luce or Congressional China-Lobbyist Walter Judd.

10 | Conclusion

The 1930s and 1940s in Chinese politics and in Sino-American relations was an extremely important period. It was the time when the Communists came to power and the American "special relationship" with China fell apart. Much of our understanding of this era is still a product of the reporting done by American correspondents. The Scottsdale get-together afforded a unique opportunity to add an in-depth, behind the scenes, dimension to what we already know about the war years in China. But what about the more general question asked in the preface: how well and effectively did American journalists report on a non-Western society in the throes of drastic, revolutionary change?

At Scottsdale only "old hand"-turned-historian John K. Fairbank attacked this question frontally and with force:

All that is now basic to reporting on, say, France or Russia or any part of the world was lacking on the Chinese scene. There was nobody you could talk to, even if you went to the academic research centers, who could really tell you what the situation in the countryside was. We had no knowledge, in other words, and no way to gain any knowledge, of the life of ordinary Chinese people. The Communists were in touch with them and working on them as best they could, and yet they themselves didn't know too much. They were finding methods of organization and of violence and of indoctrination that would work, but it wasn't on a basis of knowing all the facts.

Today, the historians that I read are looking at the domestic Chinese situation: the state of the Chinese family in the process of twentieth-century industrialization; the state of peasant livelihood in a society where urbanization is at work and the peasant is getting the short end of market arrangements. All of these domestic factors are what social scientists and such are writing about voluminously.

So the modern historical profession is going back to the conditions of life of the common people and presenting us with a scenario that says the Revolution was in the cards. The Japanese destroyed any chance that the Nationalists might have led in another way. The Nationalists had to become military in response to the Japanese. In any case, the Nationalists probably never had enough of a base among the common people to do the job. Until that leadership of the villages and mobilization of the villages could be achieved, there was to be no other alternative; everybody would be waiting around, hanging fire, making do, and not getting into the new China of the future. In this sense the Chinese Revolution is a hundred-year-long process.

This, of course, reflects on all of us who were in the government or in the press and reporting as best we could. Our reporting was very superficial. As has been pointed out, it was mainly through the English language, it was seldom from a village, and I don't recall ever talking to a peasant in the three or four years that I was in wartime China. I think we have to see ourselves as rather small and thin, a stratum on the surface of things and in no position to assert what were the basic movements that are now beginning to be documented.

Every journalist is walking on a fault line—of unresolved and ambivalent historic situations—trying to represent it some way in words. It is probably the essence of the journalistic profession, as I understand it from the outside, that reporters deal with ambivalent situations where the outcome is uncertain, the values are mixed, and the sides are in conflict. This still goes on today. It is the hopeful sign of our present situation that we seem to have come to terms with the Chinese Revolution after about forty years. We have, after forty years, accepted history to a certain degree. . . .

[Thus] from the point of view of history, this reunion should be a wake. The American experience in China (during the 1940s) was a first-class disaster for the American people. I need not argue, perhaps, that the wars in Korea and in Vietnam are part of this disaster. It's perfectly plain that we all tried, but we failed. Everybody here participated in one of the great failures in history. I mean that we could not educate or illuminate or inform the American people or the American leadership in such a way that we could modify the outcome. We are the creatures who will be examined in retrospect as having been around; we struggled but we didn't succeed.

Regardless of point of view, there is consensus today that the big story of the 1940s in China did not occur in Chungking. It was taking place in the countryside. Politically a dramatic shift in control of population and territory (between the Kuomintang and the Communists) was underway. It is clear from the record that this story was not dealt with adequately in the US press.[1] This is the failure of which John Fairbank spoke.

Other Scottsdale participants side-stepped the issue and were more self-congratulatory in their overall assessments. "We did a damn good job," was the benediction offered by Henry Lieberman. In a letter to the conference organizers, Teddy White excused the superficiality of their work with the argument that it was inevitably so because China was then and remains today inscrutable.

We were all very young men, ignorant men, unskilled men. China was a mystery to all of us, as it remains to this day a mystery to the most learned scholars. We never knew who was doing *what* to *whom* or *why.* We could not penetrate Chinese politics. We lived on the slope of a volcano; we could see it steaming, record an eruption now and then, knew the landscape was heaving, and all of us sensed that this volcano would blow its top.

This mystery of China was a mystery not only to us, but to the leaders of China, too. Chinese scholars, I have come to conclude, have the greatest sense of chronology. But chronology is not history; and they, like us, seek still to understand what happened and is happening. China was a mystery to those of us who reported it; it remains a mystery.

As for specific factors which explain the inadequate coverage of the struggle for power and fundamental changes taking place in the Chinese countryside, the problems of censorship in the field and gatekeeping at home have been discussed. Downplayed by others but emphasized by Fairbank was the lack of language facility in Chinese and consequent reliance upon English-speaking urban-oriented sources and assistants. The latter raises a basic question about the background and training of most China correspondents in the 1940s. Com-

pared to other foreign correspondents posted elsewhere in the world, how deficient was their background?

To answer this question, a comparative profile of the China correspondent of the 1930s and 1940s is most instructive. As reference points we use an excellent study of American correspondents who covered Europe in the mid-1950s and a more recent work on those who covered Latin America during the late 1970s.[2]

The importance to the China correspondents of the University of Missouri School of Journalism has already been noted. Moreover, a significant number of China correspondents were born in the Midwest and shared rural backgrounds. This contrasts sharply with European correspondents, among whom the eastern United States was the most common place of birth. (The majority of the wire service reporters in Europe, however, were born in the Midwest.) Most Latin American correspondents were educated in eastern colleges and universities. (No data is given on their birthplaces.) In general, college educations seem to have been more common among the European and Latin American corps, but this is in part a reflection of societal trends in the 1950s and later.

A large number of the China journalists arrived in China as if "by accident" in a footloose and unencumbered manner. Steele, Isaacs, Durdin, Belden and Ravenholt immediately come to mind, and there were others as well. The European journalists, on the other hand, arrived with an academic background which could be applied to covering complex foreign issues. They were better educated, displayed relative stability in their day-to-day lives, and most brought with them larger than average families. Such "purposefulness" also prevailed among Latin American reporters. The contrast in style to

China correspondents highlights the relatively romantic nature of reporting in wartime China, an observation made repeatedly throughout the conference. There was romantic Hankow, the uniqueness of Chinese life, the special charm of Chou En-lai and, above all, the fondness that most journalists expressed for China and its people. Most of the Latin American and European correspondents, on the other hand, professed more interest in journalism as a profession than they did in the region they were covering.

This brings us back to the language issue and the question of how important it is to be conversant in the native language of a region. The consensus among the China reporters was that knowledge of Chinese was not a mandatory requirement for a good journalist. Although it could be a useful tool, a good reporter could perform at a quality level without it. This attitude reflected the prevailing lack of fluency in Chinese among those present. This stands in stark contrast to the European and Latin American correspondents. Well over half the foreign correspondents in Europe claimed to understand the oral and written language of the region at the level of "fair" or "well." The number of reporters in Latin America who claimed at least a reasonable command of Spanish or Portuguese was over ninety percent. Two explanations for this disparity are the difficulty of the Chinese language and the fact that it is a non-Western language. There was also a minimal concern among employers in the 1930s and 1940s with foreign language expertise. It has become increasingly common since World War II for managing editors to require fluency in the language of the country to which a correspondent is posted. The exception remains Asia. Few Vietnam War correspondents knew Vietnamese and in 1986 two out of roughly fifty US correspondents stationed in Tokyo spoke or read Japanese.[3]

Thus while it is true that a command of the native tongue is no substitute for journalistic skills, the inability to communicate in Chinese reinforced the urban orientation of many Western journalists in the 1930s and 1940s. To the extent that reporters remained in the cities and did not communicate directly either with peasants in the countryside or with the Communists, their ability to uncover and analyze the forces reshaping China was limited. The comment made during the conference suggesting that the Chinese-speaking commoner possessed no real insight into what was happening was revealing. Such a statement ignores the value of overhearing bits and pieces of conversation on street corners and during the normal workaday routine of ordinary people. Complaints and comments gathered in this way help a perceptive reporter to determine moods and undercurrents of social change. The diplomatic reports of John S. Service, for example, who was one of the few fluent Chinese speakers among the Americans in Chungking, are today recognized as classics of the period.[4] Clearly, therefore, the importance of speaking and reading Chinese was underrated by most of the journalists at the conference. Language deficiency was a major factor contributing to their failure to cover adequately the big story taking place in the countryside.

On the other hand, the analytical depth of the American journalists in China was improved by the activities and publications of the Institute of Pacific Relations (IPR). The IPR was an international think-tank, funded primarily by the Rockefeller Foundation, that became a target of the McCarthy-McCarran committees in 1952. In *its heyday (1925–1952), through its publications and conferences, the IPR brought together from around the world the best minds to study problems of contemporary Asia, including China. Despite the presence at Scottsdale of an IPR veteran, Dorothy Borg, the question of the Institute's influence received scant attention. Admittedly, its influence is difficult to pinpoint. Yet IPR publications and conferences provided journalists with essential background materials, and in the field they often exchanged views and sources with IPR scholars like Borg, Owen Lattimore, T. A. Bisson, Ch'en Han-sheng, William Holland, and others. Moreover, senior China journalists like Steele, Durdin, and Snow published analytical articles in IPR journals and attended its conferences. Recently the role of the IPR in helping to produce by the 1940s a core of American diplomats who were second to none in terms of China experience has been acknowledged.[5] Similar recognition should be given to the essential supportive role played by the IPR in assisting American reporting on China to reach its most sophisticated level.*

Were women reporters more prevalent in China than elsewhere? The conference participants seemed not to think so. Yet, of those attending the conference, between twenty and twenty-five percent were women who had done at least some reporting. More than ten additional names of women reporters were recalled by various attendees, adding up to a total of twenty or so. When it is noted that the American correspondent population during the war years was not more than two hundred, it becomes obvious that women made up at least ten percent of the total population of American journalists who covered China. This is more than twice the proportion of women journalists in Europe in the mid-1950s, who made up less than four percent of the American correspondent population. Although no data was given, the proportion of women reporting from Latin America seems to have been equally low. This suggests that women reporters were indeed more prevalent on the China scene than elsewhere and is best explained by China's place on the periphery of the world stage from the point of view of editors back home.

The level of censorship and gatekeeping with which the China correspondents contended seems to have fallen within a "normal" range, especially considering wartime conditions. The journalists in Europe generally (i.e., slightly more than half) felt that they had never been compelled to color their stories to correspond with the editorial policies of their employers. Nevertheless, many did agree that certain stories would often go unreported if the journalists suspected that the editorial gatekeepers would place it next to the classified ads. Neither China- nor Europe-based reporters received many direct orders from their editors. On the surface they were pretty much on their own.

But like counterparts in Europe and Washington, China reporters were a community. They met frequently and avidly clipped each other's work. During the Chung- king period in fact they even lived together in a Kuomin- tang-run press hostel. Through such interaction, consen- sus was reached about legitimacy of sources. Together they decided what was news or what should be reported and how. As suggested in chapter 3 about the Hankow "gang," group dynamics or the process of self-monitoring probably was more important to the selection and design of news reporting than censorship or gatekeeping from the outside.

Was the level of collaboration between the press and government officials unusually high in China? We have already seen that Harrison Salisbury did not think so. His opinion conforms with the sentiment expressed in a recent (i.e., mid-1970s) article on diplomatic reporting in Western Europe.[6] In it the author focuses on the "buddy system" that exists between certain correspondents and the diplomats. He points to numerous instances of mutual cooperation, such as a reporter being told not to pay too much attention to official statements during certain delicate negotiations, since real progress was being made behind the scenes. Diplomats also rely on the journalists' contacts. The author concludes that such intimacy, when properly employed, can lead to more informed and higher quality reporting.

What about partisanship and objectivity? Were the China journalists influenced more by political points of view than their counterparts in Europe? From the 1920s until the 1940s there were many correspondents in Europe who were politically active, and usually of a leftist persuasion. This attitude peaked in the late 1930s. There were, nevertheless, many who considered themselves quite detached from politics. By the mid-1950s, journalists expressing a leftist bias in their reporting had practically disappeared from the scene. This is not to say that the correspondents' own views became right-wing. For example, an overwhelming majority favored the traditionally liberal notion of reducing trade tariff barriers, and the journalists in Latin America tended to oppose American intervention in the affairs of other nations and to favor a policy of détente between the East and West. As a whole, this is not too different from the points of view of the China journalists who attended the Scottsdale conference. It should be noted, however, that there were journalists in wartime China who were right of center. Joseph Alsop, who supported Chiang Kai-shek and Claire

Chennault, in opposition to Stilwell, immediately comes to mind. And of course there was Henry Luce. Indeed, the number of American journalists who leaned to the right in China may have been disproportionately greater than those posted elsewhere in the world at the time.

James Reston and others have observed that American foreign correspondents are trained to report events and do this efficiently and well. They are weak, however, in reporting important intellectual and ideological trends in the country to which they are posted. No doubt much of the blame for this tendency lies with the demand for "hard news" by gatekeeping editors back home. This characterization certainly seems to apply as well to China reporting of the 1930s and 1940s. With the events of the Sino-Japanese War as their dominant focus, the China journalists rarely dealt with the crypto-Fascist quality of Kuomintang ideology or with political currents within the Chinese Communist movement. For example, the important Communist rectification (cheng feng) movement of 1944 was completely missed. And later, the student protest movements of the late 1940s were also poorly understood and rarely reported upon.[7]

To sum up, the China press corps had much in common with American foreign correspondents serving elsewhere in the world. What was distinctive about them was their personal background and approach to their work. China reporters tended to come to China almost "by accident" and from the Midwest. The number of women correspondents was relatively high. And, except for the few who were children of missionaries, they lacked language background or much formal training about the region. This last point goes a long way toward explaining why the grass roots decline of the Kuomintang and the rise of the Communists to power in the countryside was inadequately covered.

But the most striking difference of all between the China correspondent and contemporaries posted elsewhere in the world was the deep, emotional attachment for China that was developed on the job. The China journalist of the 1930s and 1940s felt far more integrated into the fabric of Chinese life than was true for Eastern Europe, Latin America, and the Soviet Union (as noted by Harrison Salisbury). Most China reporters unabashedly identified themselves with Chinese causes, especially those concerning Japan. Finally, the freedom of movement that they enjoyed in China further distinguished their experience and doubtless contributed significantly to the development of affection for the country.

The journalists who gathered in Scottsdale are of the generation who consciously pursued "objectivity" as journalists. They saw themselves as neutral observers of the Chinese scene, trying to be objective in the gathering of facts. But inevitably the news they reported was selective—severely limited as they were by language, access, background, official lies, censorship, and demands of gatekeepers back home. The result was a highly structured news reality or set of facts about China which meshed well with the interests of American policy and opinions about China at home. Until the mid-1940s, coverage focused on the war against Japan and Chiang Kai-shek and the Nationalists. The rise of the Communists was neglected. Then, increasingly, after the war had ended and the debate over China heated up, they created a web of facticity about the situation in China that was ambivalent and contradictory. As such it was used as ammunition by both sides in the debates that unfolded in Congress over China policy from 1945 to the White Paper of 1949.[8]

Given this symbiotic relationship between China reporting in the field and American policy and public opinion at home, the question of the influence of China reporters becomes difficult to answer. A comparative perspective only confirms that a negligible direct influence was the norm. Moreover, even to pose such a question, as was done in the preface, now seems naive. As Jack Belden commented in a post-conference interview, to think that the press might have altered America's policy toward Chiang Kai-shek is to suffer from "delusions of grandeur."

In chapter 9 we took the question a step further and concluded that the American journalist was more often than not a pawn in government maneuvers—be they Washington's, Chiang Kai-shek's, or Chou En-lai's. Discussed at length was the dynamics of this process at the time of Stilwell's recall in 1944 and later at the time of the State Department's White Paper. Similarly in terms of influencing American public opinion, the China reporter was ineffectual except as a tool in the hands of opinion-makers like Henry Luce.

Today the question of the policy influence of the foreign correspondent in Asia has been raised again in terms of Vietnam War–period coverage. The political right's use of the press as a scapegoat for the loss of a war has a remarkable parallel in the "loss of China" controversy and attacks on the press of the early 1950s. There are other parallels as well. Both the Vietnam and China reporters suffered from deficiencies of language and background. There was also an apparent correspondence between the tone of coverage in the field and changes in US policy. A careful look at the Diem period, for example, reveals this. It was clearer still at the time of the Tet offensive of 1968. At the outset, Robert McNamara resigned as Secretary of Defense, leaving American policy in serious disarray. Thus, the ambivalent, contradictory, and sometimes inaccurate coverage by the media of the Tet offensive tended to reflect the confusion reigning in Washington over policy, just as it had twenty years earlier in relation to China. Thus considering the parallels, questions of media influence in respect to Vietnam-era policies might be fruitfully pursued by using a perspective like that applied to China reporting in this book.[9]

Interestingly enough, there is also a Chinese dimension to the influence question which was not discussed at Scottsdale. Throughout the 1940s, translations of a great deal of Western reporting on China appeared in the Chinese press, including the Communist press. Lieberman, Durdin, Steele, and the like had many Chinese readers of whom they were largely unaware. For example, on June 19, 1945, the Communist Liberation Daily (Chieh-fang jih-pao) published on its front page a translation of a column by Drew Pearson about Ambassador (to China) Patrick Hurley's interview with Stalin. The main point was that the Russians—Stalin in particular—did not consider the Chinese Communists as real Communists, nor did he think that they had much chance of winning a civil war. Therefore, it was preferable for Russia to support Chiang Kai-shek over the Communists. Accompanying the column was another article carefully stating the reverse: that Stalin was Yenan's best friend. Clearly, an important message was being conveyed indirectly. The Western story was used to express what the Chinese editors feared was true about Russian attitudes but did not *want to state directly.*[10] *Thus, in yet another way, the 1940s American news report about China was used as a pawn in a larger game.*

Finally, the personal attacks for the "loss" of China made during the 1950s on many of the reporters and diplomats who gathered in Scottsdale are a reminder of Mark Twain's dictum: "It is by the goodness of God that in our country we have those three unspeakably precious things: freedom of speech, freedom of conscience, and the prudence never to practice either of them."

By now the absurdity of making this generation of China reporters into scapegoats for failures of government policy should be clear. The tragedy is compounded by the knowledge of even greater suffering on the Chinese side. In both America and China, the bearers of bad news, or those who would not be prudent, became the victims of a witch hunt. Bill Powell, himself a McCarthy period victim, made the point eloquently with a parable about Mac (McCracken) Fisher and Liu Tsun-ch'i.[11]

Mac Fisher was the United Press correspondent in Chungking at the time of Pearl Harbor. Shortly thereafter the American ambassador persuaded Mac to head up an official information service in China, which later became the Office of War Information (OWI). Chris Rand and I and a number of others were sent out from Washington early in the war to help Mac.

When we got there, he already had a fairly decent operation going. He had hired some Americans locally, such as Graham Peck, and had put together a good Chinese staff.

Heading it was an extremely able young Chinese newspaperman named Liu Tsun-ch'i. Tsun-ch'i worked for OWI throughout the war and in the early post-war period came to the United States on a fellowship. He returned, worked for a while with OWI's successor, the United States Information Service, and then returned to Chinese newspaper work.

When the Chinese Civil War ended, Tsun-ch'i became an information official in the new Communist government (unbeknownst to Fisher, he had been a Communist since the 1930s). And, as I learned later, he was one of a group of modern Chinese newsmen who urged reform of the old-style Chinese journalism.

At the end of World War II, Mac Fisher continued working for the American Government as an information specialist in the State Department. When Senator McCarthy attacked the State Department, claiming that it was subversion within the Department which had caused the United States to "lose" China, State caved in and agreed to conduct a loyalty investigation of its employees.

The investigators eventually came to Mac. He had been an important figure in the wartime American establishment in China. Was it possible that he had been a secret Communist sympathizer? He had hired Liu Tsun-ch'i as his chief Chinese editor and Liu had later become an important official in the Communist government.

It would have been impossible for Mac, or anyone else, to have explained to Senator McCarthy that almost the entire Chinese intellectual establishment had eventually opted for the Communist side in the civil war. Years of bad government had lost the Nationalists the support of the peasants, the middle class, and the intellectuals. The country was run by and for a feudal elite whose only solution to the nation's problems was to return to the Confucian verities and inequalities of the past.

In the months that followed, Mac covered page after page, putting down his thoughts, searching his memory for explanations of every major act during the previous half-dozen years. Finally, he was cleared—sort of. It was accepted that he was not a Communist, but there were still some unresolved doubts, at the least he had been guilty of poor judgment. He wasn't fired, but was barred from holding any policy-making position.

In the mid-1950s the Chinese Communists launched the first of their witch hunts. Liu Tsun-ch'i was brought up on charges of subversion and disloyalty. It was a fact that he had worked for the American Government and was known to be friendly with many American newsmen. It was also known that he had worked closely with the "American imperialist agent," Mac Fisher.

Tsun-ch'i was labeled a "rightist," fired from his job, and sent to a forestry camp for "labor reform." After a few years he was released from the labor camp and assigned to an obscure interior post as librarian. Shortly thereafter, Mao launched the "cultural revolution" and Tsun-ch'i was hauled back to Peking for further examination. This time he went to prison. Altogether, he spent some twenty years in exile and disgrace.

I saw Tsun-ch'i in Peking two years ago. He had been rehabilitated and is the founding editor of *China Daily*, the English-language paper published by the Chinese Government. And again, he is one of the leaders in an effort to reform Chinese press practices, to promote investigative journalism, and to give Chinese reporters more freedom to function as their society's watchdog.

The tragedy goes beyond the ruined careers of Mac Fisher, an American who understood China, and Liu Tsun-ch'i, a Chinese who understood America.

If irrationality had not prevailed, they, and many others like them on both sides, might have succeeded in lessening the hostility between China and America and the estrangement would not have lasted for nearly twenty-five years. If this had been the case, we might have avoided two costly and futile wars on the Asian mainland.

Ignorance is expensive, and those who try—and sometimes succeed—in shaping the news to fit their own narrow interests do their countries a great disservice.[12]

Bill Powell's story and final message is a reminder that, despite shortcomings, the 1930s and 1940s represented the highest quality of American reporting on China before or since. Diversity of viewpoint was a major reason. Today the China correspondents are few in number and live only in Peking. Hardly young adventurers like Durdin, Fisher, or Steele, or advocates like Millard, Luce, and Smedley, they are usually mid-career professionals from similar backgrounds (often including years of language and academic study). In Peking they live isolated lives, just as cut off (probably more so) from the Chinese peasant as their counterparts were in the 1940s. Stringers are rare. The result is a highly homogeneous view of China in the American media.[13] Much attention continues to be paid to the exotic and to the inscrutability of Chinese politics. Gone is the romance of the 1930s and 1940s, but the myth of a mysterious China that perturbed Professor Fairbank is perpetuated. What is needed today is to find ways to combine the diversity of viewpoint and resulting complexity of vision, which were the strength of earlier China reporting, with the years of language study and academic background which the present generation brings to the job.

200   Conclusion

Notes

PREFACE

1. Notable recent works are Gaye Tuchman, *Making the News: A Study in the Construction of Reality* (New York: Free Press, 1978); Dan Schiller, *Objectivity and the News* (Philadelphia: University of Pennsylvania Press, 1981); Harvey L. Molotch and Marilyn Lester, "News as Purposive Behavior," *American Sociological Review* 39:101–12 (1974), "Accidental News: The Great Oil Spill," *American Journal of Sociology* 81:235–60 (1975); Herbert J. Gans, *Deciding What's News* (New York: Pantheon Books, 1979).

INTRODUCTION

1. An earlier version of this general account of what happened at Scottsdale was published in *Nieman Reports*, 37:31, 32–34 (Spring 1983).

CHAPTER 1

1. John Kobler, *Luce: His Time, Life, and Fortune* (New York: Doubleday, 1968), p. 137.

2. Luce to Vandenberg, Jan. 12, 1948, in John K. Jessup, ed., *The Ideas of Henry Luce* (New York: Atheneum, 1969), p. 191.

3. W. A. Swanberg, *Luce and His Empire* (New York: Charles Scribner's Sons, 1972), p. 24.

4. *Ibid.*, p. 24.

5. *Ibid.*, p. 29.

6. Jessup, *Ideas of Henry Luce*, p. 30.

7. *Ibid.*, p. 10.

8. *Ibid.*, p. 7.

9. Speech at Centennial of Lake Forest College, Illinois, March 25, 1957, in Jessup, *Ideas of Henry Luce,* pp. 320–323.

10. Jessup, *Ideas of Henry Luce,* p. 11.

11. *Ibid.,* p. 11.

12. *Ibid.*

13. Remarks at dinner for *Time* editors, Nov. 14, 1952, Jessup, *Ideas of Henry Luce,* p. 70.

14. Robert T. Elson, *Time, Inc.: The Intimate History of a Publishing Enterprise, 1923–1941* (New York: Atheneum, 1968), p. 25.

15. Speech to the "Senior Group" of *Time* editors, writers, and executives, May 4, 1950, Jessup, *Ideas of Henry Luce,* p. 380.

16. *Ibid.,* pp. 89–90.

17. Swanberg, *Luce and His Empire,* p. 225.

18. Jessup, *Ideas of Henry Luce,* p. 190.

19. Theodore H. White, *In Search of History: A Personal Adventure* (New York: Harper & Row, 1978), p. 211.

20. Jessup, *Ideas of Henry Luce,* pp. 378–380.

CHAPTER 2

1. Edgar Snow, *Journey to the Beginning* (New York: Random House, 1958), p. 31.

CHAPTER 3

1. Freda Utley, *Odyssey of a Liberal* (Washington, D.C.: Washington National Press, 1970), p. 207.

2. Agnes Smedley to McCracken Fisher et al., no date, Fisher Papers, Arizona State University.

3. Fisher Papers.

CHAPTER 5

1. For an affectionate personal portrait of these middle-of-the-road intellectuals that recognizes their importance, see John K. Fairbank, *Chinabound: A Fifty-Year Memoir* (New York: Harper & Row, 1982).

2. On the Democratic League figures, see Suzanne Pepper, *Civil War in China: The Political Struggle, 1945–1949* (Berkeley and Los Angeles: University of California Press, 1978).

CHAPTER 7

1. For more information on Hurley's campaign against the Foreign Service officers, see E. J. Kahn, Jr., *The China Hands: America's Foreign Service Officers and What Befell Them* (New York: Penguin, 1976).

2. Barbara Tuchman, "If Mao Had Come to Washington: An Essay in Alternatives," *Foreign Affairs* 57 : 44 (October 1972).

3. For more detail on the *cheng feng* movement, see Mark Selden, *The Yenan Way in Revolutionary China* (Cambridge, Mass.: Harvard University Press, 1971), pp. 188–200, and Frederick Teiwes, *Politics and Purges in China* (White Plains, N.Y.: M. E. Sharpe, 1979), pp. 64–78.

CHAPTER 9

1. For details on the loan and US government motives, see Michael Schaller, *The United States Crusade in China, 1938–1945* (New York: Columbia University Press, 1979), pp. 96–98.

2. James Reston, *The Artillery of the Press: Its Influence on American Foreign Policy* (New York: Harper & Row, 1966), p. 63.

3. See Lyman P. Van Slyke, ed., *The China White Paper, August 1949* (Stanford: Stanford University Press, 1967) and Robert P. Newman, "The Self-Inflicted Wound: The China White Paper of 1949," *Prologue* 14 : 141–56.

4. See especially Richard W. Steele, *Propaganda in an Open Society* (Westport, Ct.: Greenwood Press, 1985), pp. 97–125.

CHAPTER 10

1. Tom Englehardt, "Long Day's Journey: American Observers in China, 1948–1950," in *China and Ourselves*, edited by Ross Terrill and Bruce Douglass (Boston: Beacon Press, 1969), pp. 90–121.

2. Theodore E. Kruglak, *The Foreign Correspondents: A Study of the Men and Women Reporting for the American Information Media in Western Europe* (Geneva: Libraire E. Droz, 1955; reprint, Westport, Ct.: Greenwood, 1974), and John C. Pollock, *The Politics of Crisis Reporting: Learning to Be a Foreign Correspondent* (New York: Praeger, 1981).

3. On Vietnam War correspondents, see Harrison Salisbury, ed., *Vietnam Reconsidered: Lessons from a War* (New York: Harper & Row, 1984); figures on Tokyo correspondents from Prof. George Packard, private communication, February 3, 1986.

4. See Joseph Esherick, ed., *Lost Chance in China: World War II Dispatches of John S. Service* (New York: Random House, 1974). Language deficiency and lack of background produced a failure of much greater dimensions in Japan where American journalists during the mid-1930s seriously misjudged the intentions and capabilities of the Japanese war machine. See Ernest May, "U.S. Press Coverage of Japan, 1931–1941," in Dorothy Borg and Shumpei Okamoto, eds., *Pearl Harbor as History: Japanese-*

American Relations 1931–1941 (New York: Columbia University Press, 1973), pp. 511–32.

5. Christopher Thorne, *Allies of a Kind: The United States, Britain and the War against Japan, 1941–45* (New York: Oxford University Press, 1978).

6. W. Phillips Davison, "Diplomatic Reporting: Rules of the Game," *Journal of Communications* 25 : 138–46 (Autumn 1975).

7. James Reston, *The Artillery of the Press: Its Influence on American Foreign Policy* (New York: Harper & Row, 1966); the *cheng feng* campaign of 1944 is discussed earlier in the text, see chapter 7; on the student movement, see Suzanne Pepper, *Civil War in China* (Berkeley and Los Angeles: University of California Press, 1978).

8. The pioneering work on journalists of this generation is Leo C. Rosten, *The Washington Correspondents* (New York: Harcourt, Brace and Company, 1937); and of foreign correspondents, Bernard C. Cohen, *The Press and Foreign Policy* (Princeton, N.J.: Princeton University Press, 1963). Recent works by sociologists are cited in the Preface. For analysis of China debates in Congress, see Kenneth Chern, "Politics of American China Policy, 1945: Roots of the Cold War in Asia," *Political Science Quarterly* 91 : 631–47 (Winter 1976–77), and Nancy Tucker, *Patterns in the Dust: Chinese-American Relations and the Recognition Controversy, 1949–1950* (New York: Columbia University Press, 1983).

9. The best work to date on Vietnam War journalists is Harrison Salisbury, ed., *Vietnam Reconsidered*; the book that originally stirred up the controversy is by Peter Braestrup, *Big Story: How the American Press and Television Reported and Interpreted the Crisis of Tet in 1968 in Vietnam and Washington* (Boulder, Colorado: Westview Press, 1977). At the Scottsdale conference and in the Salisbury volume it is evident that a generation gap exists between the veteran Asia correspondents from the 1940s and the younger journalists of the David Halberstam or Peter Arnett variety. The older generation views the younger as sensationalist and arrogantly ignorant about Asia. Bridging the gap are veteran Asian correspondents who arrived in the 1950s, like Stanley Karnow and Robert Shaplen.

10. *Chieh-fang jih-pao*, June 12, 1945. This practice in the Chinese press—of using a foreign story about China to make a domestic political point—has continued to this day. *Reference News (Cankao xiaoxi)*, which has a daily circulation of over eight million, is a compendium of translated news stories produced by the New China (*Xinhua*) News Agency. The selection

is understood by the Chinese public to convey political points that are often different from what the foreign writer intended. Observation based on author MacKinnon's two years in Peking, 1979–1981, working with the *People's Daily* and the New China News Agency.

11. For additional data on Liu, see Harold R. Isaacs, *Re-encounters in China* (Armonk, N.Y.: M. E. Sharpe, 1985), pp. 95–110.

12. Excerpted from a paper read by Bill Powell at a University of Montana conference on "The China Hands' Legacy," April 19–20, 1984. Quoted with permission from conference organizer, Charles Hood.

13. Recently a new generation of American China reporters, able to be *in situ* in Peking for the first time since 1949, have produced remarkably similar books in terms of viewpoint and conclusions about China. Two even have the same title. See Fox Butterfield (*New York Times*), *China: Alive in the Bitter Sea* (New York: Times Books, 1982); John Fraser (*Toronto Globe*), *The Chinese: Portrait of a People* (New York: Summit Books, 1980); David Bonavia (*Times* of London), *The Chinese* (New York: Lippincott and Crowell, 1980); Jay and Linda Mathews (*Los Angeles Times*), *One Billion: A China Chronicle* (New York: Random House, 1983); and Richard Bernstein (*Time*), *From the Center of the Earth: The Search for Truth about China* (Boston: Little, Brown, 1982).

Glossary

PERSONS

Abend, Hallett

(1884–1955) *New York Times* correspondent stationed in China and Japan during the 1930s and 1940s.

Atkinson, Brooks

(1894–1984) Correspondent for the *New York Times* and one of the visitors to Yenan in 1944.

Bao Dai

Emperor of Vietnam until 1945, supported by the French and Japanese, and Head of State of South Vietnam until 1955.

Buck, J. Lossing

(1890–1975) Agriculture and economics expert on China; married to Pearl Buck.

Chambers, Whittaker

(1901–1961) *Time* Foreign Editor; former Communist turned rabid anti-Communist by 1940s.

Chang Hsueh-liang	(1898–) Son of Chang Tso-lin and warlord of Manchuria who kidnapped Chiang Kai-shek at Sian in 1936.
Chen, Eugene	(1878–1944) Foreign Minister for Nationalist government at Hankow in 1927.
Chennault, Claire	(1880–1958) Major General in command of "Flying Tigers" and U.S. 14th Air Force; strong supporter of Chiang Kai-shek and opponent of General Stilwell.
Chiang Mon-lin (Meng-lin)	(1886–1964) American-educated Chinese liberal and university president during Sino-Japanese War.
Chiang T'ing-fu	(1895–1965) American-educated scholar and diplomat; in 1940s, director of political department of Executive Yuan in Chungking.
Donovan, "Wild" Bill	(1883–1963) Major General William J. Donovan, in charge of OSS during WWII.
Dorn, "Pinky"	Brigadier General Frank Dorn, an aide and confidant to Stilwell.
Fei Hsiao-t'ung	(1910–) Chinese sociologist and anthropologist.
Fu Ssu-nien	(1896–1950) European-

educated Chinese liberal and head of Academia Sinica during Sino-Japanese War.

Goldman, Emma

(1869–1940) Reformer and anarchist in early 1900s.

Gordon, "Chinese"

Charles George Gordon, a British army officer who served as an officer in the Chinese army during the Taiping Rebellion in the 1860s.

Hu Shih

(1891–1962) Leading Chinese reformer and liberal; ambassador to US during WWII.

Huang Hua

(1912–) English-speaking 1936 student leader who migrated to Yenan and worked for Chou En-lai; became foreign minister in 1980s.

Hurley, Patrick

(1883–1963) Ambassador to China and a leading accuser of the China-specialist Foreign Service officers in 1945 and 1946.

Lattimore, Owen

(1900–) Businessman, newspaperman, traveler, and scholar of China and Inner Asia; target of McCarthyism in 1950s.

Lin Piao

(1907–1971) Communist general who died after allegedly plotting a coup against Mao Tse-tung.

Ma Yin-ch'u

(1882–1982) Western-trained

	economist, demographer, and educator who publicly criticized the Kuomintang in the 1940s.
Miles, "Mary"	(1900–1961) Rear Admiral Milton E. Miles, coordinator of OSS in the Far East and founder of SACO; opponent of Stilwell and avid supporter of Chiang Kai-shek.
Nelson, Donald	(1888–1959) American industrialist and official in FDR's administration.
Robertson, Walter	Virginia banker and pro–Chiang Kai-shek official in the State Department during the civil war period.
Soong Mei-ling	(1897–) Maiden name of Mme. Chiang Kai-shek.
Soong, T. V.	(1894–1971) Sung Tzu-wen, brother-in-law of Chiang Kai-shek as well as finance and foreign minister during 1940s.
Stennes, Captain Walther	Chiang Kai-shek's German chief of bodyguards in the 1930s.
Stilwell, Joseph	(1883–1946) General Joseph W. Stilwell, the ranking American officer in China during most of WWII.
Sun Tzu	(fl. 500 B.C.) Chinese military strategist.

Tong, Hollington	(1887–) Tung Hsien-kuang, Chinese Nationalist Minister of Information; graduate of Missouri School of Journalism.
Willkie, Wendell	(1892–1944) Defeated by FDR in 1940 presidential election; visitor to China during a round the world tour as presidential envoy in 1942.
Yeh Chien-ying	(1898–) Chinese Communist general active in Chungking during WWII.
Yen, James	(1893–) Yen Yang-ch'u, American-educated Chinese Christian and leader of rural reconstruction movement in China during early 1930s.

TERMS

Amerasia	American journal specializing in Asian affairs published during early 1940s.
Boxer Rebellion	A violent anti-foreign rebellion in 1899–1900 during which a number of Westerners were killed, causing an allied occupation and sacking of Peking and Tientsin.
China Lobby	A loose amalgam of Chiang Kai-shek supporters from China and America who became convinced in the mid-

1940s that American support for Chiang was inadequate and who later charged the US government with "losing China" to the Communists.

Chinese Civil War	The war between the Chinese Nationalists and the Chinese Communists (1945–1949).
Democratic League	An association (1944–1947) of Chinese liberals who tried to steer a middle course between Chiang Kai-shek and the Communists.
G-2	The military intelligence sections of the US Army.
Gimo	Generalissimo Chiang Kai-shek.
Happy Valley	A sabotage training center near Chungking run by Mary Miles and the Chinese Nationalists.
Hump	The Himalaya mountain range, separating China from Burma and India, over which Allied supplies had to be air-lifted.
IWW	Industrial Workers of the World.
Japanese Greater East-Asia Co-Prosperity Sphere	Japan's version of the Monroe Doctrine making all of East Asia the domain of the Japanese Empire.

Ledo Road	Road connecting India and China, built under Stilwell's leadership, that was to replace airlifts over the Hump.
Lend-Lease	The Lend-Lease Act of 1941, whereby FDR was authorized to lend military supplies to any country deemed vital to US interests.
Lytton Commission	Formed by the League of Nations and author of a report, accepted by the League in 1933, finding Japan at fault for the fighting in Manchuria.
McCarthy-McCarran Hearings	A series of anti-Communist hearings conducted by Senators Joseph R. McCarthy and Patrick McCarran in 1950–1952.
"Mr. X"	An article written by George F. Kennan in 1947 that explored US-Russian relations, signed anonymously by a Mr. X.
New Life Movement	A campaign launched by Chiang Kai-shek in 1934 to improve behavior, manners, and the quality of Chinese life in the spirit of Confucianism.
OSS	Office of Strategic Services, formed in 1942 as a covert in-

	telligence and military operations unit for the US.
OWI	Office of War Information, formed in 1942, whose primary mission was the gathering and dissemination of information related to the war effort in China.
SACO	Sino-American Cooperative Organization, headed jointly by Mary Miles of the US Navy and the Kuomintang head of secret police, in charge of numerous anti-Communist guerrilla training camps.
Salween Campaign	The campaign in 1944, led by Stilwell, to seize control of northern Burma from the Japanese in order to allow completion of the Ledo Road.
United Front	A policy of cooperation between the Chinese Communists and the Kuomintang, formed in response to Japan's attack on China in 1937 and lasting, nominally, until 1945.
UNRRA	United Nations Relief and Rehabilitation Administration, in charge of sending material supplies to wartorn China.
USIS	US Information Service, created in 1946 as a peacetime

successor to the OWI information program.

Yalta Conference   A conference held in the Soviet Crimea (February 1945) attended by FDR, Winston Churchill, and Joseph Stalin, at which several decisions were made regarding the status of postwar China.

Yenching University   The most prominent of numerous Chinese Christian colleges, Rockefeller-supported and located on the site of today's Peking University.

Selected Additional Readings

Barnett, A. Doak. *Communist China and Asia*. New York: Random House, 1961.

Barrett, David. *Dixie Mission*. Berkeley: University of California Press, 1970.

Belden, Jack. *China Shakes the World*. New York: Harper, 1949.

Borg, Dorothy and Waldo Heinrichs, eds. *Uncertain Years: Chinese-American Relations, 1947–1950*. New York: Columbia University Press, 1980.

Carlson, Evans Fordyce. *Twin Stars of China*. New York: Dodd, Mead, 1941.

Chennault, Claire L. *Way of a Fighter: The Memoirs of Claire Lee Chennault*. New York: G. Putnam's Sons, 1949.

Cohen, Bernard C. *The Press and Foreign Policy*. Princeton: Princeton University Press, 1963.

Cohen, Warren I. *The Chinese Connection: Roger S. Greene, Thomas W. Lamont, George E. Sokolsky and American-East Asian Relations*. New York: Columbia University Press, 1978.

Davies, John Paton. *Dragon by the Tail: American, British, Japanese, and Russian Encounters with China and One Another*. New York: Norton, 1972.

Engelhardt, Tom. "Long Day's Journey: American Observers in China, 1948–1950." In Bruce Douglass and Ross Terrill, eds., *China and Ourselves*, pp. 90–121. Boston: Beacon Press, 1969.

Esherick, Joseph W., ed. *Lost Chance in China: The World War II Dispatches of John S. Service*. New York: Random House, 1974.

Epstein, Israel. *The Unfinished Revolution in China.* Boston: Little, Brown, 1947.

Fairbank, John K. *Chinabound: A Fifty-Year Memoir.* New York: Harper & Row, 1982.

Fairbank, Wilma. *America's Cultural Experiment in China, 1942–49.* Washington, D.C.: Government Printing Office, 1976.

Fetzer, James A. "The Case of John Paton Davies, Jr." *Foreign Service Journal* 54 : 15–22, 31–32 (November 1977).

Gans, Herbert J. *Deciding What's News: A Study of CBS Evening News, NBC Nightly News, Newsweek, and Time.* New York: Pantheon Books, 1979.

Hamilton, John Maxwell. "The Missouri News Monopoly and American Altruism in China: Thomas F. F. Millard, J. B. Powell, and Edgar Snow." *Pacific Historical Review* 55 : 27–48 (February 1986).

Hartman, Carl. "There's a Lot of *There* out There." *The Quill* 70 : 14–16, 19–20 (December 1982).

Isaacs, Harold R. *Re-encounters in China: Notes of a Journey in a Time Capsule.* Armonk, New York: M. E. Sharpe, Inc., 1985.

———. *The Tragedy of the Chinese Revolution.* London: Secker & Warburg, 1938; rev. ed., Stanford: Stanford University Press, 1951.

Jessup, John K., ed. *The Ideas of Henry Luce.* New York: Atheneum, 1969.

Kahn, E. J., Jr. *The China Hands: America's Foreign Service Officers and What Befell Them.* New York: Penguin Books, 1976.

Keeley, Joseph C. *The China Lobby Man: The Story of Alfred Kohlberg.* New Rochelle, New York: Arlington House, 1969.

Kobler, John. *Luce: His Time, Life and Fortune.* New York: Doubleday and Company, 1968.

Koen, Ross. *The China Lobby in American Politics.* New York: Harper & Row, 1972.

Kruglak, Theodore E. *The Foreign Correspondents: A Study of the Men and Women Reporting for the American Information Media in Western Europe.* Geneva: Libraire E. Droz, 1955; reprint ed., Westport, Connecticut: Greenwood Press, 1974.

Levine, Stephen. "A New Look at American Mediation in the Chinese Civil War: The Marshall Mission and Manchuria." *Diplomatic History* 3 : 349–75 (Fall 1979).

Melby, John. *The Mandate of Heaven: Record of a Civil War, 1945–49.* Toronto: University of Toronto Press, 1968.

Newman, Robert P. "The Self-Inflicted Wound: The China White Paper of 1949." *Prologue* 14:141–56 (Fall 1982).

Nimmo, Dan D. *Newsgathering in Washington.* Englewood Cliffs, New Jersey: Prentice-Hall, 1964.

Peck, Graham. *Two Kinds of Time.* Boston: Houghton, Mifflin, 1950.

Pepper, Suzanne. *Civil War in China: The Political Struggle, 1945–1949.* Berkeley: University of California Press, 1978.

Pollock, John C. *The Politics of Crisis Reporting: Learning to Be a Foreign Correspondent.* New York: Praeger, 1981.

Powell, J. B. "Missouri Authors and Journalists in the Orient." *Missouri Historical Review* 41:45–55 (October 1946).

———. *My Twenty-five Years in China.* New York: Macmillan, 1945.

Powell, John [William]. "Special Report: My Father's Library." *Wilson Library Bulletin,* March 1986, pp. 35–37.

Rand, Christopher. "Reporting in the Far East." In Louis M. Lyons, ed., *Reporting the News,* pp. 303–12. Cambridge, Massachusetts: Harvard University Press, 1965.

Reston, James. *The Artillery of the Press: Its Influence on American Foreign Policy.* New York: Harper & Row, 1966.

Rosten, Leo. *The Washington Correspondents.* New York: Harcourt, Brace and Company, 1937.

Schaller, Michael. *The United States Crusade in China, 1938–1945.* New York: Columbia University Press, 1979.

Schiller, Dan. *Objectivity and the News: The Public and the Rise of Commercial Journalism.* Philadelphia: University of Pennsylvania Press, 1981.

Schuman, Julian. *Assignment China.* New York: Whittier Books, 1956.

Selden, Mark. *The Yenan Way in Revolutionary China.* Cambridge, Massachusetts: Harvard University Press, 1971.

Service, John. *The Amerasia Papers.* Berkeley: Center for Chinese Studies, 1971.

Shewmaker, Kenneth E. *Americans and Chinese Communists, 1927–1945: A Persuading Encounter.* Ithaca, New York: Cornell University Press, 1971.

Smedley, Agnes. *Battle Hymn of China.* New York: Alfred A. Knopf, 1943.

Snow, Edgar. *Journey to the Beginning.* New York: Random House, 1958.

————. *Red Star Over China*. New York: Random House, 1938.

Steele, A. T. *The American People and China*. New York: McGraw-Hill, 1966.

Steele, Richard W. *Propaganda in an Open Society: The Roosevelt Administration and the Media, 1933–1941*. Westport, Connecticut: Greenwood Press, 1985.

Stein, Guenther. *The Challenge of Red China*. New York: Whittlesey House, 1945.

Strong, Tracy B., and Helene Keyssar. *Right in Her Soul: The Life of Anna Louise Strong*. New York: Random House, 1983.

Swanberg, W. A. *Luce and His Empire*. New York: Charles Scribner's Sons, 1972.

Teiwes, Frederick. *Politics and Purges in China: Rectification and the Decline of Party Norms, 1950–1965*. White Plains, New York: M. E. Sharpe, 1979.

Tozer, Warren W. "The Foreign Correspondents' Visit to Yenan in 1944: A Reassessment." *Pacific Historical Review* 41: 207–24 (May 1972).

Tuchman, Gaye. *Making News: A Study in the Construction of Reality*. New York: Free Press, 1978.

Tucker, Nancy Bernkopf. *Patterns in the Dust: Chinese-American Relations and the Recognition Controversy, 1949–1950*. New York: Columbia University Press, 1983.

Utley, Freda. *Last Chance in China*. Indianapolis, Indiana: Bobbs-Merrill, 1947.

Van Slyke, Lyman P., ed. *The China White Paper, August 1949*. Stanford: Stanford University Press, 1967.

White, Theodore. *In Search of History: A Personal Adventure*. New York: Harper & Row, 1978.

White, Theodore, and Annalee Jacoby. *Thunder Out of China*. New York: William Sloane Associates, 1946.

Index

BLUM (continued)
  of the American Containment
    Policy in East Asia, xvi
Borg, Dorothy, xvi, 54, 84, 189;
    United States and the Far East-
    ern Crisis of 1933–38, xvi
Bosshard, Walter, 42
Boxer Rebellion, xxii, 11, 16, 23,
    210
Briggs, Walter, 56
Buck, J. Lossing, 144–45, 206
Buck, Pearl, 206; The Good Earth,
    120
Buddhism, 62, 65
Buell, Walter H., 10
Bulganin, Nikolay, 90
Burke, Jim, 61; My Father in
    China, 59
Burma, xix, xxii, 56, 165, 213. See
    also Ledo Road
Butterworth, Walt, 176
Byrnes, Secretary of State James
    F., 114

The Call (Socialist daily), 41
Calvinism, 13, 18
Caraway, General Paul, 145
Carlson, Evans, 42, 46
Casberg, Dr. Melvin, 148
Catholicism, 18, 71
Censorship, 103–17, 190, 193;
    American, 51, 79, 111–12, 157,
    160, 164, 167, 169; Chinese, 51,
    68, 79, 163, 165, 185; and Stil-
    well recall, 158, 161, 163, 165,
    181
Central News, 107
Chamber of Commerce, Ameri-
    can, 98
Chambers, Whittaker, 4–5, 7,
    18–19, 20, 120, 130, 138, 167,
    206
Chang Hsueh-liang, 27, 207
Chang Tso-lin, 27, 207
Cheeloo University, 10
Chefoo School, 10, 15
Chen, Eugene, 57, 207
Ch'en Chia-k'ang, 103

cheng-feng campaign of 1944,
    147, 148, 192
Ch'en Han-sheng (Chen Han-sen),
    56–57, 189; Landlord and
    Peasant in China, 56
Chennault, Claire, xv, 166,
    191–92, 207
Chiang Kai-shek (Gimo), 7, 21,
    40, 113, 136, 195, 207; army of,
    121; arrest at Sian, xxviii, 207;
    and censorship, 103, 107;
    China's Destiny, 107; in
    Chungking, 48, 50, 51; and
    Communists, 46, 134, 141, 157,
    167, 211; and journalists, 27,
    93, 138, 151, 155, 158, 191, 193,
    194; New Life Movement of,
    212; and Stilwell, 159–68; sup-
    porters of, 209, 210–11; and US,
    142, 152, 194
Chiang Kai-shek, Mme. (Soong
    Mei-ling), 4, 6, 9, 17, 27, 50, 79,
    80, 91–93, 120, 209
Chiang Mon-lin (Meng-lin), 93,
    207
Chiang T'ing-fu, 93, 207
Chiang Wei-kuo, 107
Chicago Daily News, xv, xxiii,
    xv, 134, 139, 174
Chicago Sun Times, xxi
China: "special relationship" of
    US with, 182; Japanese in, 48,
    100, 132, 171; journalistic pro-
    cess in, compared with Soviet
    Union, 128–32; and Korean
    War, 174; Lend-Lease to, 161,
    168; "loss of," xxx, 134, 194,
    196, 197, 211; peasants in, 98,
    145, 182–84, 188, 199; press of,
    195, 198; US public opinion
    about, 120–26, 128, 131–32,
    134, 149–56, 169, 172, 181;
    women correspondents in,
    52–55, 189–90, 192
China-Burma-India Theater, xxii,
    xxiii, xxix, 56, 160
China Daily (Peking), xxiv, 198
China Defense Supplies, xv

China Forum, 33
China Lobby, xxx, 9, 181, 210–11
China Press, xxii, xxiv, 25, 33
China Reconstructs, xvii
China Weekly Review (Shanghai), xxii, xxiii, xxiv, xxvi, 25, 26, 54, 61, 112–13
China Welfare Institute, xxii
China White Paper, xxi, xxx, 169, 175, 176–77, 178, 179–81, 194
Chinese Communists, xxviii; and editors, 138; Eighth Route Army of, 41; guerrilla bases of, 48; and intellectuals, 197, 198; journalistic bias toward, 6, 149–56, 191–92; and journalists, 6, 41, 49, 73, 79, 84, 88, 92, 94, 97, 101, 188, 192, 193; and Korean War, 174; and Nationalists, 20, 37, 46, 66, 84, 134; New Fourth Army of, xxix, 57, 103–4, 174; news blockade of, xxvii, xxix; and newspapers, 152, 195; and party line, 85, 88; and peasants, 65, 105, 183, 184; and Russia, 83, 84–85, 86, 147, 167, 168; and US, 85, 86, 161
Chinese Industrial Cooperatives, 9
Chou En-lai, 38, 65–66, 79, 92, 93, 103, 136, 194; accessibility of, 3, 40, 49; effect on correspondents of, 3, 65, 80–86, 88–89, 187; and New Fourth Army Incident, 104; and Soviet Union, 86, 89–91; and Yumen oil fields, 106
Christian Science Monitor, xvii, xxii, 56, 57, 69, 134, 159; "Inside the War," 104–5; on recall of Stilwell, 111, 163
Chungking, 17, 110, 114, 207, 210; Chinese capital moved to, xxviii, 32, 36, 48, 137; Chou En-lai in, 40, 79, 83, 84, 92; falsified information from, 60, 81–82, 92; Japanese bombing of, 51–52; journalists in, xvii, xviii, xxvii, 3, 4, 20, 55, 57, 64,

68, 91, 102, 103, 119; as news center, 32, 108, 145, 171, 190, 196; US officials in, xix, xxiv, 80, 141, 176; women correspondents in, 52–55
Churchill, Winston, 214
Civil War, Chinese, xxviii, xxx, 5, 146, 152, 162, 164; and intellectuals, 197; press coverage of, 1, 7, 60, 67, 134; US involvement in, 166, 168, 178, 209; view of Stalin on, 195. See also Chinese Communists; Nationalists
The Coast, 59
Cold War, 5, 119, 134, 152–53, 155
Colgate University, 34
Columbia Broadcasting System (CBS), xxi
Columbia University, 101
Communism, 18–19
Compass, xvii
Confucianism, 197, 212
Congress, US: and appropriations for China, 114, 172, 181; and journalists, xxx, 172, 181, 194; and Korean War, 178
Connors, Bradley, 70
Correspondents, American: comparative profile of, 186–93; and editors, 118–40, 190, 192, 193; in Europe, 186–87, 190–91, 193; influence of, 169–81, 194; and intellectuals, 101; in Latin America, 186, 187, 190, 191, 193; women, 52–55, 189–90, 192
Crane, Charles, 24

Davies, John Paton, xvi, 7, 9, 11, 13, 69, 70, 143; and China White Paper, 179; Dragon by the Tail, xvii
Davis, Consul Monnet B. (Shanghai), 154
Davis, Elmer, 63
Deane, General John R., 76–77
Deane, Hugh, xvii, 44, 56–58, 103–5

de Gaulle, Charles, 87
Democratic League, 93–94, 211
Diplomats, 5, 7, 168, 177, 178,
189; and journalists, 67–78,
179, 191. *See also* China White
Paper
Dixie Mission. *See* Army, US:
Observer Group of
Domei News Agency, 19, 63, 137
Donovan, William J. (Wild Bill),
45, 207
Dorn, Frank (Pinky), 115, 116
Doyle, Ann, 54
Doyle, Bob, 54
Dulles, John Foster, xvii
Durdin, Peggy, xvii, 51–52, 54, 55,
56, 80–81, 150
Durdin, Tillman, xvii, 32–34, 43,
52, 58, 136, 199; and American
officials, 67, 173, 174; arrival in
China, 32–33, 56, 130, 186; and
China White Paper, 180–81;
and Chinese press, 195; on
Chou En-lai, 80, 83–84; in
Hankow, 38–40; on interpret-
ers, 97; and IPR, 189; on Kuo-
mintang sources, 93

Ebener, Charlotte, 55, 72
Eddy, Sherwood, 10
Epstein, Israel, xvii, 4, 35–36,
122, 136, 178; and Belden, 44;
on censorship, 105–8; on
knowledge of Chinese lan-
guage, 100–101
Eskelund, Karl, 106–7

Fadiman, Annalee Jacoby, xviii,
xxvii, 50–51, 122, 145; on Ambassador Hurley, 5–6, 141–44;
on Chinese language, 95; on
Mme. Chiang Kai-shek, 91–92;
on Whittaker Chambers, 138;
and women correspondents,
53–54, 55
Fadiman, Clifton, xviii
Fairbank, John K., xviii, 100; on
anti-Communism, 152–53; on
Chinese Revolution, 183–84;

on knowledge of Chinese language, 102–3, 185; and OWI,
64, 67–68, 113; on reporting
from China, 6, 182–84, 199;
The United States and China,
xviii
Fairbank, Wilma, xviii, 94; *A Pic-
torial History of Chinese Ar-
chitecture*, xviii
Far Eastern Survey, 159
Farnsworth, Clyde, 105
Fei Hsiao-t'ung, 99, 207
Fisher, F. McCracken, xviii,
119–20, 123–24; on altering
dispatches, 136–37; on govern-
ment manipulation of press,
171; and Hankow "Gang," 43;
and McCarthyism, 196–99; on
Mme. Chiang Kai-shek, 92; and
OWI, 58–59, 113; at Yenching
University, 27–28
Fleisher, B. W., 25
Foreign News, xx
Fortune, 15
France, 62–63, 87, 160, 206
Franco, Francisco, 38
Frankfurter Zeitung, xxv, 41
Free Press (Manila), xxi
Friesen, Oris, xix
Frumkin, Dr., 131
Fulbright Foundation, xxi
Fu Ssu-nien, 93, 207

Gauss, Clarence, 143
Geneva Conference, 89
German Transocean Agency, 63
Gibbons, Floyd, 30
Gimo (Generalissimo). *See*
Chiang Kai-shek
Goldman, Emma, 41, 208
Goldstein, Steven, xix; *China
Briefing*, xix
Gordon, Charles George ("Chi-
nese"), 162, 208
Gordon, Matt, *News as a Weapon*
by, 63
Gould, Randall, 55, 56
Government, US: and press, 5, 8,
67–78, 80, 170–81, 190, 194.

Wordsworth, William, 45–46
World Church Religious News Service, 54
World War II, 31, 60, 76, 88, 99, 113, 197, 207, 208, 209; US allies in, 158
Wuhan, 37

Yale Daily News, 14
Yale University, 11, 14, 17
Yalta Conference, 158, 214
Yangtze River, 32, 33, 37, 48, 50, 103, 146
Yeh Chien-ying, 75, 210

Yeh Ting, 57
Yen, James (Yen Yang-ch'u), xix, 210
Yenan, 121, 133, 150, 165, 167; American journalists at, xxix, 4, 19, 41, 69, 70, 105, 131, 149, 154–55, 206; American Observer Mission in, 146, 147, 148; Chou En-lai in, 79, 85, 208
Yenching Gazette, 28–29
Yenching University (Peking), xviii, xxvii, 10, 214; Department of Journalism, 27–28
Yumen oilfields, 105–6